IS YOUR DAUGHTER READY?

IS YOUR DAUGHTER READY?

10 WAYS TO EMPOWER YOUR GIRL FOR AN AGE OF NEW CHALLENGES

KARI KAMPAKIS

W PUBLISHING GROUP

AN IMPRINT OF THOMAS NELSON

Published in Nashville, Tennessee, by W Publishing, an imprint of Thomas Nelson.

Published in association with the literary agency of Wolgemuth & Wilson.

Thomas Nelson titles may be purchased in bulk for educational, business, fundraising, or sales promotional use. For information, please email SpecialMarkets@ThomasNelson.com.

Unless otherwise noted, Scripture quotations are taken from the Holy Bible, New Living Translation. © 1996, 2004, 2015 by Tyndale House Foundation. Used by permission of Tyndale House Publishers, Carol Stream, Illinois 60188. All rights reserved.

Scripture quotations marked ESV are taken from the ESV® Bible (The Holy Bible, English Standard Version®). Copyright © 2001 by Crossway, a publishing ministry of Good News Publishers. All rights reserved.

Scripture quotations marked MSG are taken from *The Message.* Copyright © 1993, 2002, 2018 by Eugene H. Peterson. Used by permission of NavPress. All rights reserved. Represented by Tyndale House Publishers, Inc.

Scripture quotations marked NIV are taken from the Holy Bible, New International Version®, NIV®. Copyright © 1973, 1978, 1984, 2011 by Biblica, Inc.® Used by permission of Zondervan. All rights reserved worldwide. www.Zondervan.com. The "NIV" and "New International Version" are trademarks registered in the United States Patent and Trademark Office by Biblica, Inc.®

Any internet addresses, phone numbers, or company or product information printed in this book are offered as a resource and are not intended in any way to be or to imply an endorsement by Thomas Nelson, nor does Thomas Nelson vouch for the existence, content, or services of these sites, phone numbers, companies, or products beyond the life of this book.

ISBN 978-1-4003-4290-7 (audiobook)
ISBN 978-1-4003-4289-1 (ePub)
ISBN 978-1-4003-4287-7 (TP)

Library of Congress Control Number: 2025932249

Printed in the United States of America

25 26 27 28 29 LBC 5 4 3 2 1

To Dad,
For your steadfast strength and wisdom.
You've blessed me in ways I can never repay.
You are my treasure too.

In most cases, we have eighteen years to prepare our daughters for life beyond our home.

Eighteen years to pack the suitcase they'll carry through life.

Here are ten essentials worth prioritizing.

ESSENTIAL #1:   LOVE

ESSENTIAL #2:   TRUTH

ESSENTIAL #3:   INTEGRITY

ESSENTIAL #4:   RELATIONSHIP SMARTS

ESSENTIAL #5:   PERSPECTIVE

ESSENTIAL #6:   DISCERNMENT

ESSENTIAL #7:   CONNECTION

ESSENTIAL #8:   PURPOSE

ESSENTIAL #9:   PERSEVERANCE

ESSENTIAL #10: FAITH

CONTENTS

INTRODUCTION

God gave us our children so we could
prepare them to be adults.

BILLY GRAHAM

My family has a running joke about my suitcase on vacation. In short, it's always heavy. It's a mystery whether my bag will exceed the fifty-pound weight limit at airport check-in.

Last Christmas I was gifted a luggage scale to avoid the embarrassment and the hassle. Sadly, we've been that family who has had to step aside, open our bags, and redistribute the weight that I carry. Typically, my shoes go first, as shoes are the worst offender when it comes to weighing my luggage down.

My husband, Harry, has gotten smart in staying ahead of this problem. He packs lightly and leaves room in his carry-on for items that I may need to transfer.

Harry and I have been married for twenty-seven years, and this explains why. He knows me well and leaves that extra space even when I promise that I've packed better.

Because the truth is, I start off strong. I'm intentional when I begin to pack as I prioritize the essentials. But as our departure time approaches, I haphazardly cram things in. I overpack and make my bag heavy, creating a beast too big to carry.

In many ways, I believe, parenting can follow a similar trajectory. We haphazardly cram things in as our child's departure time approaches. We panic, stuff, and overpack.

In most cases, we have eighteen years to pack the suitcases our daughters will carry through life. We have eighteen years to raise them and prepare them as best we can for life beyond our homes—and life as legal adults.

In the beginning, when our girls are young, it's easy to focus on the essentials. We carefully pack their suitcases with love, security, and warm memories.

We have eighteen years to pack the suitcases our daughters will carry through life.

But as our girls grow up, a sense of urgency kicks in. We see the harsh realities of this world, and it can kick us into overdrive as we try to prepare them and make up for all the ways we think we missed the boat.

What we once considered *essential*—like love, faith, and character—can get buried or lost in the shuffle as we aimlessly pack during their final years at home.

Overpacking may look like:

- being overly critical;
- micromanaging their lives;
- expecting perfection;
- sharing too many corrections at once;

- sharing too many life lessons at once;
- forcing a love for God on them;
- controlling their relationships and decisions;
- obsessing over their social lives;
- overscheduling them;
- living vicariously through them;
- raising the daughter we *want*, not the daughter we *have*; and
- parenting with a vision of gloom and doom rather than a vision of hope.

Before we know it, we've made their suitcases heavy. We've transferred our baggage (our worries, fears, regrets, or shame) into our daughter's suitcase and created a beast too heavy to carry. What should be their toolbox to navigate life suddenly feels like a burden to unload.

A burden they may leave behind as they leave our home.

I may overpack when it comes to vacations, but when it comes to parenting my four daughters, I want to be intentional. I want to save my energy for what matters most, wisely discerning what belongs in their suitcase . . . and what belongs in mine.

Even more crucial than the life skills our daughters will need to be healthy adults (skills like housekeeping and doing laundry, which can be picked up quickly) is the moral compass that will guide them. This compass develops over time through the values we pack, the choices they make, and the experiences they have.

This compass also impacts their life direction. It helps them choose a healthy road—the road that leads to God. Our girls will make mistakes, but I want my daughters to know *when* they've made a mistake. I want them to journey with self-awareness so that one wrong turn doesn't lead to more wrong turns away from their Creator.

After all, the safest place to be is in the middle of God's will. As C. S. Lewis wrote, "To walk out of His will is to walk into nowhere."[1]

Thankfully, the Lord is ready to help. He partners with us to prepare our girls. He wants to lighten our load and relieve us from feeling like their future depends entirely on us.

Just as my husband leaves extra space in his suitcase to take on my excess load, God leaves extra space too. *Only, God's space has no limits!* He has an endless capacity to take on our burdens. He redistributes the weight we carry.

This truth matters because in my twenty-two years of parenting, motherhood has never felt so heavy. Dark realities weigh us down as we try to love, guide, and protect our daughters in an age of new challenges—and a society that's drifted far from God.

The stress can feel crippling, but what keeps me going is a heightened awareness of what girls today will face. They need strong mothers, fathers, and mentors. They need guidance from healthy adults who care about their journey.

My friend, this book is designed to empower *you* as you empower and champion your daughter. It's an optimistic yet realistic guide to the paradox of our broken world. A world where we try to raise our daughters in the light—yet prepare them for the dark. A world that is hungry for hope despite the heartache and pain we see.

When my friend Laura works in her garden and pulls up all the weeds, she is often reminded that we're *not* living in Eden. We haven't made it to paradise yet. One day we'll enjoy heaven, but until then, we're in this messy middle place. We have people to love, truths to instill, and hope to restore through Jesus.

Our daughters are being shaped by a culture that is darker, meaner, and more complex than the culture that shaped you and me. They face adult-sized problems at a younger age and many trials unique to their generation.

The good news is, God has blessings in store for our daughters. It's important to remember these truths:

- He created your daughter for this moment in time.
- It's no accident that she is here (or that you've been chosen as her mom).
- God designed your daughter to serve her generation like no one in the universe has ever served before. She is here to know Him and advance His kingdom!
- Even when she loses faith in herself, she can have faith in the Lord. His strength is her protection.
- Bigger challenges for her generation equal more opportunities for spiritual growth at a younger age. Your daughter has great potential to surpass you in faith, and when the one you've poured into begins to outrun you, it's a cause for celebration.

As a mom of four girls, I'm in the trenches with you. I have one daughter in graduate school, two daughters in college, and one daughter at home. I know the worries in your heart.

I've made *many* mistakes, and that may be my best qualification to help you. By sharing what I've learned through personal experience plus thousands of interactions with moms and girls today, I hope to elevate your clarity and confidence.

You can't control the world, but you do have agency inside your home. You can model and instill what you hope to see. For that reason, this book focuses on what you can do at home. It's designed to help you build your daughter up before you send her out.

Parenting is a lifelong journey, so be patient. Don't rush the process or expect quick results. Rather than apply this whole book at once, start with what feels relevant. Focus on one chapter at a time and what your daughter needs most right now.

Even as she leaves home, your daughter will still need you. She'll still need your guidance and wisdom. Your presence and support. Your intuition and forewarnings. Don't think your chance is over just because she's almost grown. Don't assume your ship has sailed if you wish you'd packed her suitcase differently.

Regret is a heavy burden, and while we should certainly learn from the past, it's unhealthy to stay stuck there. God's mercies are new each morning, and as my friend Cynthia Yanoff said, "Today is the perfect day to stop worrying about what the world says good parents are supposed to do and instead do what we're called to do."[2] Keep moving forward by seeking the Lord. Pray for relief from the baggage that makes motherhood feel dismal or heavy.

Your longest relationship with your daughter will begin *after* she leaves home. While you have eighteen years to pack her suitcase, you parent toward the adult friendship that could last fifty years or more. Today's choices set the stage for that friendship. They help you build a relationship where your daughter wants to come to you.

Her suitcase will never be perfect, but it can be powerful. It can help her thrive, survive, and find her way back home. Getting your daughter ready for life means getting her ready for heaven. Both paths lead in the same direction, and ultimately, heaven is the light we travel toward.

Getting your daughter ready for life means getting her ready for heaven.

Our world needs your daughter, and your daughter needs *you*. May God lighten your load as you help her become a remarkable blessing to her generation.

Cheering for you,

Kari

> But those who trust in the Lord will find new strength.
> They will soar high on wings like eagles.
> They will run and not grow weary.
> They will walk and not faint.
>
> **ISAIAH 40:31**

CHAPTER 1

LOVE

PARENT HER HEART

*The gospel is this: We are more sinful and flawed
in ourselves than we ever dared believe, yet at the
very same time we are more loved and accepted
in Jesus Christ than we ever dared hope.*

DR. TIM KELLER

When my daughters were young, I had one child who was a firecracker. She had a mind of her own and an iron will, and as my brother joked, she had sparks coming off her.

Her extra energy wore me out. She constantly got into predicaments I never saw coming, like that time at the beach when she kept her hand on the elevator door as it slid into the wall and got her hand stuck in the door gap. (Thankfully, her uncle set her free!) Even as a baby at Mother's Day Out, she'd eagerly crawl outside her classroom when she heard the big kids in the hall. She loved action and adventure, and she lived her life ready to *go!*

With four kids in our family circus, I was exhausted. I loved this daughter dearly, but I needed her compliance. I didn't have time for an outlier, and I was constantly frustrated as I tried to correct her and make her obey me. My sole focus was to change her behavior.

My husband responded differently. Rather than get upset when she acted out, he stayed calm. He'd pull her aside, sit her on his lap, and quietly talk to her.

On many occasions this irritated me because I thought she needed tough love. I felt like her dad was being too soft to inspire real change.

But over time I noticed two things. One, she listened to her father and behaved better after they talked. And two, she often hugged her father for no reason at all. I envied this connection because she never came up to randomly hug me . . . and that made me question my approach.

My husband would tell me that she wanted to please us and needed a little extra attention, but I didn't buy it. In my mind she was a troublemaker, and it was my job to lay down the law and get her behavior under control.

Yet here's what happened as this firecracker got bigger: My always *correcting* her without *connecting* to her created a gulf between us. That gulf grew wider until I realized one day that I'd lose my relationship with her if I didn't course correct.

Our kids are human, and like any human, they prefer to listen to people who love them well. Yet it's hard to feel loved when all you hear is correction, scolding, or being told to get your act together. Can you relate to this? Have you ever known someone who loves to point out your mistakes and imperfections? Chances are, you do. We all know someone like this.

My daughter and I have a great relationship now, and her strong-willed nature has served her well. But if I could redo her toddler years, I would. Rather than solely parent her behavior, I'd parent her heart. I'd make her heart my top priority, seeing beyond the antics to speak to the little girl who wanted to please her parents.

I realized this several years ago as I ripped out pages of her baby book. Page after page, I had complained about how difficult she was. It never occurred to me then that maybe *I* was part of the problem.

As a young mom, I needed more patience. Rather than raise my voice and shame her in front of her sisters every time she acted out, I wish I'd taken two minutes to pull her aside, sit her in my lap, and affirm her by saying this:

"I *love* your spirited personality. God created you extra-strong, and one day, it will help you move mountains. My job is to channel your spirit, and right now, I need you to listen. I need you to obey me. If you don't listen, you'll face the consequences. I'll have to get tough, and I don't want to do that. Do you understand me?"

I'd follow up with a hug and tell her how deeply loved she was.

It always intrigued me how my daughter felt drawn to her father even after he disciplined her. The secret, I believe, is that she felt secure in his love. She trusted him and knew he had her best interest in mind.

Similarly, when we understand God's love for us, we feel secure too. We can handle the discipline and correction that we trust is for our best.

We're all wired to find love, and when we meet someone who radiates love, we crave their company. We want to please them, and even if we drift away, we're likely to gravitate back.

As mothers, we're called to model God's love and mercy. Love is the most essential thing we pack in our child's suitcase. We know how deeply we love our daughters, but do our daughters feel it? Is our love conveyed through our words, actions, and attitude?

Sometimes in our effort to raise good humans, we get so focused on "perfecting" our daughters that we forget to delight in them. We internalize their poor choices and project into the future, imagining wild scenarios—like a toddler who's out of control winding up in jail one day!

This narrative creates panic. It can make us swing too far to immediately resolve every weakness we see. In the process, we lose sight of our blessings. We start to treat our daughters like problems to be fixed rather than children to be loved. And since our kids are intuitive, they pick up on this. They know when our love doesn't feel real.

Not having *our* heart in the right place will undermine our connection with our daughters. It may lead to moments where we notice them hugging their father or someone else—but not us.

Dr. Meg Meeker said that raising a strong daughter begins by showing her you care. The key is to "stay engaged, to be there, to understand."[1] While it's easy to stay tender when our daughters are young, these tender moments can wane as they grow up. Out of frustration, fear, or anger, our hearts can harden. I always know I need a reset when I feel cold, apathetic, or checked out as a mom. These are clues that it's time to ask for God's help.

What about you? Do you ever struggle with negative feelings toward your daughter? Do you do more correcting than connecting? If so, talk it over with God. Ask for help to identify the problem. Is it perfectionism or unrealistic ideals? Is it a fear of people thinking that you're a bad mother? Is it criticism from your past that has suddenly resurfaced? Are you scared about the future—or just tired and stretched thin because motherhood feels exhausting?

Whatever it is, remember that God loves you. You can't surprise Him or scare Him away. Open your heart to His grace and pray to see yourself—and your child—through His eyes.

Do You Tell Your Daughter, "You're a Blessing"?

Many years ago, I wrote an article titled "Children Are Blessings, Not Burdens."[2] It was summertime, and my girls were fighting. I was at my wit's end, and I needed a reminder that they were good inside.

What surprised me—and saddened me—in the months that followed was how many people found my website through the Google search "children are burdens." My website analytics show that I still get visitors who discover me through this phrase.

On one hand, I get it. We all go through seasons that beat us down or distort our thinking. Throw in a crisis, sleep deprivation, trauma, or a lack of support, and motherhood can feel like punishment.

Yet even on our darkest days, children are a gift from God. They're a reward from Him (Psalm 127:3). God chose us to be their temporary guardians and to lead them well with love.

Motherhood can take us to the end of ourselves. It will test our patience, resolve, and faith. Yet rock-bottom moments can also draw us closer to God. When we're down on our knees, we're humbled. We open the door to having our hearts transformed.

This transformation strengthens us. It unlocks the Holy Spirit, God's presence in the heart of Christ believers, to help us reject the cultural lie that tells us children are burdens.

The better option is to empower our daughters as we emphatically say, "You are a *gift*, so don't let anyone convince you otherwise. Don't ever doubt your worth. I don't know what I did to deserve you, but I'll take it. I feel so lucky to be your mom!"

Your daughter can't hear this message enough. With all the negative self-talk that plays inside her head, she needs reminders of how valued she is.

Maybe you need this reminder, too, especially if you've ever been told that *you* are a burden. If so, let me be clear: That is a lie. *What is true for your daughter is equally true for you.* You are God's masterpiece, fearfully and wonderfully made (Ephesians 2:10; Psalm 139:14). What God creates, God loves; and what God loves, He loves forever. Don't let someone's inability to see your worth mess with your self-esteem. Don't let it hurt your ability to love.

Regardless of what you've been told, you set the tone in your home. You can break generational cycles of pain by flipping the script, finding good role models, and imitating God (Ephesians 5:1). A healthy family can come from you even if you didn't come from a healthy family. You can create a better future for your daughter and yourself.

Parent with Your Daughter's Darkest Days in Mind

My friend had just arrived home from the doctor when the school receptionist called. She'd forgotten to complete the back of a form, and this receptionist was angry. She lit into my friend, who was already having a terrible day.

Because at that doctor's appointment, she learned that she had breast cancer. She was still processing the news.

If the receptionist had known this, I'm sure she would have been kinder. She'd probably be mortified to realize what she'd done. Nobody wants to make a bad day worse, yet there she was, losing her mind and her temper over an incomplete form.

To me this story illustrates the state of our society, where overblown reactions to glitches and mistakes have become normalized. While it hurts to be attacked by an acquaintance, it hurts worse to be attacked by a loved one. I try to remember this when I want to unleash on my daughter because her bedroom is a mess, she's complaining about driving her sister, or she forgot to take the dog out and now the dog has peed on my rug.

Even when correction is needed, I can choose my words wisely. As Proverbs 15:23 says, "Everyone enjoys a fitting reply; it is wonderful to say the right thing at the right time!"

Not acting on knee-jerk reactions helps me parent with my daughters' darkest days in mind. It makes me think twice before I respond. Our daughters struggle with pain that we can't see, and while their problems may not be as life-threatening as cancer, they can feel overwhelming to them. What we see visibly is the tip of the iceberg, the 10 percent above the surface. But under the water line, there's more to their story. There are events and emotions our girls are sorting through.

Maybe they've been hurt, betrayed, or blindsided by a friend. Maybe their boyfriend cheated—or their ex-boyfriend found a new love.

Maybe they're being bullied.

Maybe they're fighting a tough temptation and beating themselves up for being weak.

Maybe they've been severely insulted—or told that they should just die.

Maybe someone violated their trust or their body.

Maybe they've made a mistake the whole school is talking about.

Maybe they're moody because they're exhausted from trying so hard.

We want them to tell us everything, but sometimes they're not ready. Sometimes the pain hurts too much to say it out loud. Sometimes they lack the energy to bring us into the loop. Sometimes they're so busy with school or activities that they compartmentalize their struggles to deal with them later.

We can't force our daughters to open up, but we can show support. Here are five ways to show your daughter that you're on her team:

1. **Emphasize that no problem is bigger than your love for her.** Look for chances to say, "You aren't meant to struggle alone, and you can tell me *anything*. If I ever feel unequipped to help you, then I'll find someone who can help. I promise you that."

2. **Add a journal to her bedside table and talk about the therapeutic effect of journaling her thoughts and feelings.** Learning to *write* about her struggles can help your daughter *talk* about her struggles. Journaling also allows her to reflect on her blessings, thoughts, and faith journey. Encourage

your daughter to include prayer requests in her journal so she can look back and see how her prayers got answered.

3. **Cultivate relationships between your daughter and trusted adults who she can confide in or ask for advice.** This may include her friend's mom, her aunt, her coach, her favorite teacher, her Young Life leader, her youth pastor, and so on. Whoever loves your daughter well, make sure you love *them* well. Express your appreciation by giving them a gift or writing a thoughtful note.

4. **Be proactive with your daughter's mental health by connecting her with a respected Christian counselor.** Getting her comfortable with counseling (ideally when her life is going well and the conversation is easy) removes the stigma. It establishes her as a client, which can help your daughter get an appointment faster when real issues arise. Since many counselors have a six-month wait list, this makes a difference.

5. **Wait for the right time.** Especially in adolescence, your daughter will talk on *her* terms. Be ready to drop everything when she's ready. And when she seems extra chatty, like when you're driving her home from a game and she's in a confessional mood, prolong the conversation. Take the long way home. Ask if she wants to get ice cream. Let her blare the radio with her favorite songs. Most importantly, listen more than you talk. Ask her, "Do you want my advice—or my ear?" before speaking into her situation.

Again, our daughters fight battles we know nothing about. Some days they feel like they're drowning under the pressure of school, social media, friends, boys, or worrying about their future.

We can hold them accountable without making their bad days worse. We can apologize when we overreact.

Connection is protection, and the more connected you are to your daughter, the stronger your intuition will be. Sometimes what our daughters need is a little extra warmth, grace, and affection.

Love the Daughter You Have, Not the Daughter You Want

My strong-willed toddler is now in college, and her determined nature made her easier to launch.

She was ready and excited to go, and I found comfort in remembering what I once heard about strong-willed children: *They're less likely to be talked into things they don't want to do. They're not compliant to a fault, as a people pleaser might be prone to be.*

Clearly, we can't predict how any child will handle their freedom, but in today's world, our daughters need grit. They need to feel comfortable with setting boundaries, standing up for themselves, thinking for themselves, staying true to their convictions, and not letting anyone coerce them or push them around.

What I once tried to change about my daughter is now one of my favorite traits. She's a natural leader, a hard worker, and a go-getter. I still believe she'll move mountains one day.

At her first Parents' Weekend in college, several of her close friends told me how kindhearted and beloved she is. One friend used the word *angel*, and I laughed to myself because I never imagined this little firecracker would grow up and earn that title. I wish I'd known then what I know now. I wish I'd seen her potential.

God didn't make mistakes when creating my daughters or yours. He knows that it takes all personalities to make the world go round. The closer we get to Him, the more authentic we become. He is a creative God who loves variety.

The girl who fails to make the tennis team for five years straight may become a rock-star entrepreneur who later credits her failures to building the fortitude she'd need to go the distance.

The quiet girl who rarely speaks up may become a prolific artist who expresses deep emotions that help people heal and feel seen.

The girl with a learning disability may develop an unbelievable work ethic that helps her achieve great feats and inspire others to dream big.

And the outspoken girl who isn't afraid to rock the boat may be the leader her friends need when something is wrong and someone has to speak up.

I started motherhood with preconceived notions. I saw my daughters as my second chance, hoping they'd be like me but smarter and more talented so I could help them succeed.

But guess what? My daughters are uniquely wired. While I certainly relate to them and see myself in them, I'm also aware that their lives are not my do-over.

In fact, the qualities I admire most are the ones I *don't* possess.

Parenting the heart of your daughter means letting go of your fantasies, embracing her natural bent, and helping her thrive. What traits was she born with that you can't change? How can you channel her gifts in a positive direction?

Only time will tell how God plans to use her. You can't predict the situations that will call for her strengths. A trait that feels like a terrible flaw may be a lifesaver in some cases. A devastating rejection may be protection.

Mothers and daughters often clash when their personalities differ. If you're a social butterfly, you may not understand why your introverted daughter just wants a few close friends. If you were a college athlete, you may feel frustrated that your daughter just picks daisies on the soccer field.

Yet with any personality, there is hope. There is a purpose and a plan. Rather than love the daughter you *want*, love the daughter you *have*. It's a pivotal moment when you can celebrate your daughter without wishing for her to change. It's fun to be surprised as you watch her life unfold.

Our children need guidance and correction, but first they need love and connection.

Our children need guidance and correction, but first they need love and connection.

So connect before you correct. Unlock the healing power of family. And when you feel frustrated, think twice before taking action. Remember that deep inside your daughter, there's a little girl who wants to please you.

If you're lucky, you may get some spontaneous hugs. You may find yourself on the receiving end of your daughter's affection.

Packing love in your daughter's suitcase is essential because well-loved people know how to show love. From the overflow of her heart's abundance, your daughter will be able to share what she's been given. She'll be better equipped to help others know God.

Truths Worth Packing

- "Dear friends, let us continue to love one another, for love comes from God. Anyone who loves is a child of God and knows God." (1 John 4:7)
- "Most important of all, continue to show deep love for each other, for love covers a multitude of sins." (1 Peter 4:8)
- "And I will give you a new heart, and I will put a new spirit in you. I will take out your stony, stubborn heart and give you a tender, responsive heart." (Ezekiel 36:26)
- "Love never gives up, never loses faith, is always hopeful, and endures through every circumstance." (1 Corinthians 13:7)
- "Love is patient, love is kind. It does not envy, it does not boast, it is not proud. It does not dishonor others, it is not self-seeking, it is not easily angered, it keeps no record of wrongs. Love does not delight in evil but rejoices with the truth. It always protects, always trusts, always hopes, always perseveres." (1 Corinthians 13:4–7 NIV)

Questions to Unpack

1. Name a time when you corrected your daughter but didn't connect with her—and things went south. What did you learn? What would you do differently?
2. Did you have preconceived notions of your daughter

as a baby? What's been your favorite part of watching her personality develop? What qualities do you admire most?

3. Love flows down, and just as God's love flows down to you, your love flows down to your daughter. Her love then flows down to others. Do you ever just sit with the Lord to feel His love for *you*? How might this habit influence the love you give?

A Prayer to Lighten Your Load

Dear Lord,
Help me love my daughter well, speak to her heart, and cultivate a strong connection. When she faces a struggle, give her the courage to speak up. Surround her with people who uplift her. I praise You because my daughter was carefully made in Your image. Let our home be a safe place where she feels appreciated, seen, and understood. In Jesus' name, amen.

CHAPTER 2

TRUTH

PLANT SEEDS OF TRUTH

*The goal isn't to have a Bible
collection on your shelf,
but a collection of the Bible stored up in yourself.*

WENDY SPEAKE

When my daughter was fourteen years old, she broke her finger while doing a back handspring at a gymnastics lesson one night.

Her cheerleading tryouts were scheduled for the following week, and for months she'd worked to achieve a triple back handspring pass to impress the judges. Her lesson ended quickly, however, as her finger swelled and she felt a piercing pain that required a visit to the emergency room.

The doctor on call took X-rays. And when he came back, his grim expression said it all. "Her finger is definitely broken," he said. "And she'll definitely need surgery."

We tried not to think about tryouts until the next morning, when we met with an orthopedic surgeon who specializes in athletes. She said this particular injury required surgery *that week*. She had an opening the next day, and if we confirmed by four o'clock, we could have that slot.

It was a lot to process—especially the timing. Besides my fear of surgery, I worried about my daughter missing her tryouts and needing six weeks to recover.

She was a valued member of her team. She'd worked hard to achieve her tumbling requirements, yet due to this unique situation, we had to wait and see whether she could try out once her finger healed.

Watching my daughter handle this uncertainty led to many proud moments for me. I was impressed by her faith and strength. As we talked about tryouts the night before surgery, I reminded her to brace for any outcome. I didn't want her to be caught off guard if she had to wait until the following year to try out again.

That's when she said, "I really want to try out, but if I can't, it's okay. My identity is in Christ, not in my uniform."

Well, I could have cried on the spot because I'd instilled this truth in her. I'd repeated it many times to her and her sisters—never knowing that one day, I'd need it repeated to me. In my sadness for her, I'd forgotten what I knew deep down. I'd forgotten how God comforts us when we need it most.

The summer before her injury, I'd written an article titled "10 Truths Middle Schoolers Should Know." It included this point:

Truth #4: Your uniform is not your identity. Labels are big in middle school, and there is a confidence that comes from wearing a football jersey, a cheerleader uniform, or other team attire. But remember that having a uniform—or even designer clothes—doesn't increase your worth. You're special because of who you are, not what you put on your body or what you achieve. Overnight you can lose your place on a team. You can lose your talents, your wardrobe, your relationships, even your Instagram account. But if you base your identity on the one thing you'll never lose—God's love—your foundation is unshakable. You'll still be standing even if you lose every earthly trapping this world says is important.[1]

While I believed this message as I wrote it, I didn't consider it essential. I hadn't lived through a real-life application. God prompted me to share it in advance, and on a painful night for my daughter, He called it to mind.

I realized then why Scripture is a lifeline. Why planting seeds of God's truth in a child's heart really does matter. All the Bible verses that my daughters picked up piecemeal along the way (through Bible clubs, summer camps, church, Mother's Day Out, conversations at home, and more) shaped their impressionable hearts.

Some days, I wondered if I was wasting my time. I watched my girls act bored or tune out when I read a devotional before school or took them to church. In these moments, I felt tempted to quit. I considered letting them call the shots in their faith journey.

But I didn't quit, and I'm glad I didn't, and I encourage you not to quit either. Because one day, your daughter will need God's truth. Her heart will break open, and she'll feel lost as she searches for answers.

She may look to friends, celebrities, or online gurus for help, but these searches will fall short. Nothing will satisfy the God-shaped hole in her heart quite like God Himself.

In these vulnerable moments, the seeds of God's truth that you planted in the past—seeds that sat on top of your daughter's heart and waited patiently for the right time—may suddenly sink into her broken heart. This is how the light enters the darkness. This is how God comforts your daughter in times of pain.

As parents, we're called to plant seeds of truth. We're called to surround our children with godly influences who water the seeds we've planted. God will make sure these seeds take root at a time most opportune to our child's salvation.

That timing could be tomorrow—or twenty years from now. We can't predict or control that part, but we can find peace in knowing the foundation is laid. Our girls have a lifeline of truth inside them that God can call to mind anytime.

Real truth is timeless, eternal, and unchanging. It's found solely in God because God *is* truth, the Creator of heaven and earth. Jesus is the way, the truth, and the life. No one comes to the Father except through Him (John 14:6).

We can argue with the truth, and we can disagree with the truth, but we can't *change* it. It doesn't swing with popular opinion. What was true when Jesus walked this earth is equally true today. Anything built on distorted truth won't stand the test of time.

When life feels scary, chaotic, or uncertain, God's truth is a game changer. It can bring supernatural peace as you wait for answers.

When life feels scary, chaotic, or uncertain, God's truth is a game changer. It can bring supernatural peace as you wait for answers.

Once my daughter's injury healed and she could tumble again, she was invited to try out for the cheer team. She made it, and we were grateful; but what made me most proud was knowing that she could handle any outcome. She didn't find her identity in her team or her uniform.

Life will throw curveballs as we raise our children. Even perfect circumstances can change overnight with a broken bone, a broken heart, a broken promise, or a broken relationship. Thankfully, God's promises stand. He redirects us when our plans change.

You can't go wrong in teaching your daughter Scripture. You won't regret taking five minutes to share a verse that speaks to you. One day when her heart breaks open, and you're at a loss for words, the seeds you planted earlier may finally feel relevant. They may suddenly sink in and take root.

Where Do You Find Truth?

Ten years ago, as I wrote my first book, I also wrote articles for a children's hospital. One article talked about the startling rise of adolescent eating disorders. The doctor I interviewed had just attended a conference where they talked about technology's impact.

Eating disorders have always existed, she said, but what presented new issues was the way that information gets dispersed. What was once shared in small groups, mainly girls talking with their closest friends, could reach a wider audience through social media.

Since most children don't approach the internet with a great filter, they're prone to believe what they read or see. With the right bells and whistles, any website can look legitimate. Even false, misleading, and harmful information can be packaged well and presented as truth.

One hot topic at this physicians' conference was the proliferation of online communities like Pro-Ana and Pro-Mia. While

Pro-Ana websites promote an anorexic lifestyle, Pro-Mia sites promote bulimia.

Pro-Ana sites show photos of emaciated girls that provide "thinspiration." They feature crash diets, weight loss competitions, and advice on how to suppress your hunger and skip meals without your family noticing. Pro-Mia sites offer tips on how to induce vomiting and what foods won't burn your throat when they get regurgitated. As you can imagine, these sites can lead children (and adults) down a dark rabbit role.

It pains me to think of this, yet I share this story as an example of the harmful narratives that modern-day girls get exposed to. Thanks to technology, there's no limit to the content that can quickly mislead them.

And since algorithms flood their news feeds with more of what they view, an issue like an eating disorder can quickly spiral. A girl's sense of "normal" can be warped when it appears that everyone she sees is dieting, losing weight, or obsessing over their body.

As moms, we worry about social media's impact on our girls. Yet we also see false narratives. We don't always stay vigilant in deciding who to believe. To help our daughters develop a healthy internet filter, we need one first. This means thinking twice before we accept a message—and teaching our girls to do the same.

Again, anyone can look legitimate online. Anyone can gain a following with a clever message or a great personality.

Gone are the days when stories got fact-checked for accuracy before publication. No longer is traditional media the gatekeeper of all news.

Today, we *all* have a microphone. Even amateurs can build an empire. Right or wrong, it all lands on the internet, and it's up to us to discern what is true in an age of fake news, propaganda, and information overload.

Have your daughter ask herself questions like these:

- Who do I consider a trustworthy source?
- Who has a reputation (and a history) for telling the truth?
- How do I evaluate competing ideas and news stories?
- If a video goes viral, does that make it true?
- Does popular opinion determine right from wrong?
- Do I believe everything I read and see? Do I think for myself? Do I consider the source when choosing which narrative to believe?
- Where do I go first: to God or to Google? What answers can be found online—and what requires divine wisdom?
- How is God speaking to me? What do I hear when I get still?
- Who is the expert of my life? Who is never wrong?

We've all made the mistake of trusting a human more than we trust God. We've prioritized advice from strangers over wisdom from Him.

Technology can be used for good. It can be our friend or our foe, depending on how we use it. My first book deal came about because an article I wrote went viral—and that book led to more books and a new career. It unlocked my passion to help mothers and daughters.

For this reason, I can't hate the internet. I know it's not all bad. But I also can't deny the dark underside. The internet has grown increasingly corrupt as people invent new ways to manipulate and take advantage of others. We worry about our girls, but boys have also become major targets for online exploitation and sextortion too.[2]

In addition, US Surgeon General Dr. Vivek Murthy has called the declining mental health of American children the "crisis of our time." He named social media as a driving force and said that companies that own social media platforms "aren't doing enough to address the damage they're causing" and that age thirteen is "too young" for children to access these platforms.[3]

I agree, and I'm thankful for authors like Jonathan Haidt, who recommended four new norms in his book *The Anxious Generation: How the Great Rewiring of Childhood Is Causing an Epidemic of Mental Illness*:

1. No smartphones before high school
2. No social media before sixteen
3. Phone-free schools
4. More independence, free play, and responsibility in the real world[4]

I've never heard a parent say that they wish they'd given their child a smartphone sooner than they did. Many parents wish they'd waited longer—and that includes me!

This is why I tell the moms behind me, "Wait as long as possible. Learn from my generation, the pioneers who gave our children cell phones way too early. There's more at stake now with new apps and darker content. The more mature your child is, the better equipped they'll be."

Through technology, we lose control over what our daughters see. We miss the rabbit holes they can go down. It's worth asking ourselves: *What do I want in my daughter's suitcase? Do I want it filled with tawdry TikTok videos, Instagram influencers selling a lifestyle she can't afford, and selfies? Do I want my eighth-grade daughter dying for a boyfriend or my tween daughter becoming a Sephora girl as she splurges on expensive skincare that can damage her young skin[5]—all to be more like the older girls online?*

Or, do I want to pack goodness in my daughter's suitcase first? Do I want to protect her small window of childhood and not rush growing up?

I believe in teaching our daughters to use technology wisely. Moms often use my book *Liked* for this purpose. But one thing I'd do differently, if I could parent again, is save the smartphone for high school and have tighter limits for screen time.

I'd also tell my daughters:

- "Social media apps are addictive by design. They try to maximize the time you stay on. My job is to set limits until you can set limits for yourself."
- "You *can* live your life without an audience. You'll discover more peace by not sharing every detail of your life."
- "Rarely will you feel better about your life after being on social media. Most likely, you'll feel worse. Don't be scared to take a break, delete the app, or get off social media if your heart needs it. This isn't a sign of weakness; it's a sign of maturity."
- "Pay attention to how you feel without your phone. When you're at camp or a retreat with no technology, do you feel less anxious? Are you happier with your life? Putting down your phone to engage with real-life people and create real-life memories is a choice you'll never regret. This is how real friendships grow."

- "Social media is fun, but when your head spins from too much stimulation, it's time to pull back. Tune out the human noise so you can hear God."
- "God is the expert of your life because He made you. He'll never mislead you, and unlike social media companies, which could go out of business tomorrow, His Word endures forever (1 Peter 1:25). Seek the Lord, and you'll never get lost."

It's okay to come to faith just a step or two ahead of your daughter. She benefits from watching God transform your life—and when you grow together in faith, it can be a sweet journey. The blessings work both ways.

I used to beat myself up because my faith was deeper with my fourth child than with my first child. When my oldest daughter left home, I regretted not having been a better role model of carving out quiet time. But God filled that gap by surrounding her with great influences who inspired this discipline and deepened her faith. She's a Young Life leader and very passionate about the Lord, yet I can't take the credit. Her daily quiet time isn't because of me.

God is at work even when we fall short. And while planting seeds as parents is important, we don't want to go overboard. We don't want to make faith feel like a heavy burden.

Recently I heard a story of a mom who forced her daughter to do fifteen minutes of quiet time every morning before school. Now that her daughter is on her own, she's rejecting God. She wants nothing to do with Him. Hopefully she'll come back to her faith, but one lesson we can learn in the meantime is to keep joy in the picture.

Again, God wants to *lighten* the load we carry. He helps us walk in freedom.

As you instill truth in your daughter's heart, plant one seed at a time. Be patient and trust God's timing. Take small steps like the following:

- Put a devotional on her nightstand (for little girls I recommend Wynter Pitts's books; for teen and college girls try my new devotional *Yours, Not Hers: 40 Devotions to Stop Comparisons and Love Your Life*).
- Get her a Bible she'd enjoy (for little girls I recommend *The Jesus Storybook Bible*; for older girls try *CSB She Reads Truth Bible*; *Bible for Teen Girls: Growing in Faith, Hope, and Love*; or *The Catholic Youth Bible*).
- Take her to a gospel-centered church, because for her to love God, she needs to know Him first.
- Live out your faith with joy, peace, and humility.
- Ask a ministry leader or godly friend to take your daughter out for ice cream or coffee to talk about her life and answer any questions.

God has planted eternity in the human heart (Ecclesiastes 3:11). And when we feel peace from reading or hearing Scripture, it's because He designed us to know, love, and serve Him. As Saint Augustine said, our hearts are restless until they find rest in Him.[6]

Instilling truth in your daughter gives her a standard for comparison. It counters the lies and half-truths that she'll hear. The truth speaks for itself and resonates deep in the soul. Rather than require a filter, it can become her filter. It helps your daughter decide what to believe and who to trust.

Reinforce Your Daughter's Worth

In May 2023, a documentary about sorority recruitment at a large SEC university was produced by VICE Studios. At the time, my daughter was a high school senior preparing for sorority recruitment at this university.

My heart broke as I listened to a high school senior in the film share her hopes for college. She said, "Being in a sorority will help me figure out the person I want to be. Because I feel like I don't really know who I am."[7]

For months I'd told my daughter the exact *opposite* of this message. Throughout her senior year, I'd reminded her to grow strong in her identity in Christ before she ever stepped foot on campus.

I wanted her rooted in this truth because in the real world, her identity, self-worth, and self-image would be challenged like never before. Relying on fellow eighteen-year-olds to determine your worth is a risky proposition, and I wouldn't advise anyone to depend on random people to tell them who they are.

Because our daughters will meet a mixed bag of people. Some people will lack integrity. Some people will be deceitful. Some people won't know God or have love in their heart. Some people will think only of themselves.

Pope John Paul II once said that the opposite of love isn't hate but rather *use*—"treating persons like things and things like persons," and using others for selfish desires.[8]

While every human is made in God's image, not everyone sees that. Not everyone will treat our daughters like the gifts they are. A starry-eyed girl leaving her family and home may soon be disillusioned as she experiences the worst of humanity.

It could be:

- a boy who uses her for a one-night stand;
- a former friend who shares her secrets;
- a group that labels her with a horrible nickname;
- a professor who belittles her;
- a boss or coach who abuses their power;
- multiple groups that reject her;
- social media trolls who try to destroy her; or
- a frenemy who is brutally honest.

Our daughters will encounter both angels and bullies, and, sadly, it's usually the voice of a bully that rings loudest in their heads.

Even if your daughter skips college or trade school and starts to work instead, she'll still encounter hurtful people. It could be a colleague—or a stranger. Recently I heard of a girl who was thrilled to start her first job as a television news anchor. But in her first week, as the station posted her headshot to Facebook, the backlash rolled in. People didn't like her smile, and the comments got so ugly that the station deleted the post.

Can you imagine being twenty-two and targeted with such hate? When did people decide that it's okay to publicly insult a young woman's appearance?

I don't understand it, and yet here we are, raising kids in a culture that lacks empathy, class, and standards.

We can't shield our daughters from these events. We can't predict the feedback they'll hear. But we can arm them with truth. We can keep them off the emotional roller coaster of letting humans define who they are.

After all, that is one wild ride. When we give people the power to build us up, we give them the power to tear us down too. We put ourselves at the mercy of fickle humans who can change their minds overnight.

Thankfully, there *is* a better way. There is a love letter from God in Scripture. His truth is for everyone, and whether you've heard it all your life or are just getting started, it never gets old.

Our daughters need to hear this (and maybe you do too):

- **Some people won't see you clearly. They may overlook you, mock you, or undervalue you.** But remember: People don't determine your worth—God does. He made you in His image and knew you before you were born (Genesis 1:26; Jeremiah 1:5).
- **What people say about you is their opinion. What the Lord says about you is a fact.** The way to know your worth is to focus on the facts.
- **Jesus died for you. Now you get to decide how you'll live for Him.** How will you pass on the love and grace you've been given?
- **Your beliefs will never be challenged more than when you leave home.** Stay grounded in truth, look for light, and spend time with good people. Know who deserves a place in your most trusted circle.
- **Your emotions are important, but emotions can mislead you.** Just because you *feel* insignificant doesn't mean you *are* insignificant. God made you with great intention, and nothing about you is a mistake. Every detail plays into His plan for you.
- **If you could see how God looks at you, with the smile of a

proud Father, you'd never doubt your worth again. He doesn't love you because you're good—He loves you because He's good, and nothing you do or say can change that.

Confidence comes when our daughters know their worth in the Lord. They don't need a college campus, a workplace, or any human setting to tell them who they are. All they need is the voice of truth ringing loudest in their head.

Anticipate as You Wait

My daughters and their friends all love disposable cameras.

It's funny to me how these cameras made a comeback. After all, our kids thrive on instant gratification. They aren't used to waiting—yet they anticipate *this* wait. They love the suspense of wondering what unscripted moments they caught on film.

The truth is, we all love a good surprise, don't we? We don't mind waiting if we know a reward is coming. As a teenager, I loved the thrill of this wait as well. There was always a highlight photo that made the wait worthwhile.

Sometimes as moms, we wait impatiently. We wonder why it takes so long for our lessons to hit home. We try packing virtues in our daughter's suitcase (messages about joy, kindness, generosity, and compassion), but we're not sure that they sink in. When our girls act bored or seem unreceptive, we wonder if we've wasted our time.

Meanwhile, all around us, we see quick transformations. We watch television shows where people get a new life, a new house, or a new body in six weeks or less. But real life isn't so neat and linear. Real-life transformations can sometimes feel painfully *slow*.

Will we wait impatiently for our seeds to sink in—or will we anticipate what God may do? Can we find peace by doing our part and leaving the timing to Him?

Seeds that are planted can't be unplanted. My friend found comfort in these words from her counselor as her daughter left home. Like many moms, she wondered: *Have I taught her enough? Prepared her enough? Done enough? Said enough? What if I left something out?*

Nobody can steal what you instill in your daughter. Even if your wisdom sits dormant for now, it's ready for retrieval. God can call it to mind anytime.

Your daughter's heart is hungry for direction, and she's listening to you even when she acts like she isn't. Giving her a biblical worldview now can set the stage for spiritual maturity.

Dr. George Barna, in his book *Raising Spiritual Champions*, said a person's worldview is largely in place by age thirteen. Adults typically reach the end of their lives with the same worldview they had at thirteen. Most parents, however, don't plan for their child's spiritual formation. They outsource their child's worldview development to "experts" with dismal results.[9]

Dr. Barna's call to strategically disciple our children to think and live like Jesus is crucial. While I wish I'd had this book as a young mom, I also know it's not too late. I'm still shaping the worldview my daughters will carry through life—and so are you.

Planting seeds of truth *is* discipleship. It transmits your faith to the next generation. You never know how just one Bible verse may help your daughter down the road:

- When she feels frustrated by her lack of progress in the physical therapy required after a bad accident, she may remember when you told her not to get tired in doing what is good because at the right time, she'll reap a harvest of blessing (Galatians 6:9).

- When she feels devastated by a loss, she may remember when you told her the pain that she feels today can't compare to the joy that's coming (Romans 8:18).
- When a mean girl starts a rumor about her, she may remember when you told her that God can use for good what man means for evil (Genesis 50:20).

The examples are endless because God's creativity has no limits. He constantly finds new ways to raise our hearts and minds to Him.

Share God's truth with your daughter as it applies to everyday conversations. Store up a treasure in her heart. God is writing a story through her life that includes every high and low, and though you can't predict the curveballs, you can feel confident that many truths you share today will circle back around to help her.

Packing truth in your daughter's suitcase is essential because one day down the road, she'll need it. Her heart will break open, and she'll desperately long for guidance. In these moments, the good seeds you planted (or someone else planted) may sink in and become her lifeline. They may illuminate her darkest seasons and show her the path of hope.

Truths Worth Packing

- "These commandments that I give you today are to be on your hearts. Impress them on your children. Talk about them when you sit at home and when you walk along the road, when you lie down and when you get up." (Deuteronomy 6:6–7 NIV)

- "Jesus answered, 'I am the way and the truth and the life. No one comes to the Father except through me.'" (John 14:6 NIV)

- "They traded the truth about God for a lie. So they worshiped and served the things God created instead of the Creator himself, who is worthy of eternal praise! Amen." (Romans 1:25)

- "This means that anyone who belongs to Christ has become a new person. The old life is gone; a new life has begun! And all of this is a gift from God, who brought us back to himself through Christ. And God has given us this task of reconciling people to him." (2 Corinthians 5:17–18)

- "And I am certain that God, who began the good work within you, will continue his work until it is finally finished on the day when Christ Jesus returns." (Philippians 1:6)

Questions to Unpack

1. Do you believe God's truth can be a lifeline? Why or why not?
2. It's okay to come to faith just a step or two ahead of your daughter. If you're not sharing Scripture already, what verse can you share this week? What can you write on a Post-it Note to stick on her bathroom mirror?
3. What drives your daughter's confidence? How much power does she give to what people say and think? How might instilling God's truth strengthen her identity and self-worth?

A Prayer to Lighten Your Load

Dear Lord,
Guide me as I teach my daughter. Let the good seeds I plant come to mind when she needs them. Sharpen her judgment to know which voices to trust. When she doubts herself or hears harsh criticism, guard her heart. Instill an armor that comes from knowing You. I praise You for the peace and clarity found in Scripture. What a joy to find solace in You. In Jesus' name, amen.

CHAPTER 3

INTEGRITY

TEACH HER TO BE A LIGHT

*Nothing can dim the light which
shines from within.*

MAYA ANGELOU

It was tenth grade, and my daughter's class was experiencing friend shifts.

I was already feeling emotional from watching her turn sixteen. Something about this milestone birthday—and calculating how close sixteen is to *eighteen*, meaning just two more birthdays at home—left me crying for months.

Mentally, it was a rough time for me. As I imagined the future, I could only see loss. I imagined walking around an empty home looking sad, dazed, and confused with all my children gone.

My mother's health issues didn't help matters much. I was losing the security of that relationship, and with so many life changes at once, I spent a lot of time praying and figuring out my grown-up roles.

The tenth-grade friend shifts were largely due to the changing social scene. In every circle, there were fissures: Some girls wanted to drink, and some girls didn't. Some girls wanted to attend parties with seniors, and others preferred a low-key night at someone's home.

Girls were branching out in different directions, yet nobody wanted to leave their established friend group for fear of having no place to go.

What I've learned since then is how common this dynamic is. Very few girls make it through high school without a friend shift or a lonely season somewhere along the way.

Even if partying isn't the issue, another issue comes into play: girl drama, personality clashes, power struggles, a new leader, a fight over a boy, old friends drifting apart, or another variable.

Our daughters' relationships can have less security than we like to believe. As moms, we have to make peace with that. People change and dynamics evolve, and we can't be scared for our daughters to leave a group that's no longer a good fit.

Even when things get bad, many girls stay with the wrong friends. They settle for less than they deserve just to have weekend plans. Their decisions are fear-based.

But our daughters will never find the courage to be their best selves if their friend group isn't healthy. Whatever their friends do, they're likely to follow suit.

In my daughter's case, two friends had merged with a wilder crowd. The group texts were getting darker as several girls fixated on how much they hated their lives and just wanted to get drunk on Friday night. I had valid concerns, and so did the mother of my daughter's best friend. Our girls didn't see the writing on the wall. They didn't want to leave their group.

As this mom and I met for coffee, we expressed gratitude that they had each other. We knew to tread carefully because teenagers are tricky. Speak too bluntly, and they'll get defensive. Be a dictator, and they may rebel. Make someone the forbidden fruit, and they'll only want that relationship more.

We knew that subtle was the way to go, yet we weren't sure of the next best step. That's when the other mom said: "I'm just praying for light to find light." Immediately, these words resonated with me. This became my prayer too.

Over time, this issue worked itself out. Turning sixteen proved to be a blessing as my daughter could meet other friends for lunch, shopping, or a walk. She also started to date a boy who occupied more of her time.

As she saw her friend group less, they naturally parted ways. They remained friendly and on good terms. There was no bad blood among them.

Senior year brought a great surprise as she and her best friend merged with a fantastic group. I couldn't have asked for a better finale to her high school years.

Yet this story could have played out differently if she'd never branched out. The combativeness in her personality that I was starting to see would have snowballed.

It's true that the light shines best in the darkness. Our daughters can reflect God's goodness in any group or setting. But in their most formative years, when they just want to fit in, where they become rooted matters. Being a light can feel juvenile or embarrassing when the environment isn't conducive. Mentioning Jesus can create an awkward silence when your friends couldn't care less about faith and already make you feel intimidated.

I've seen girls hide their light and lose their confidence because they're surrounded by the wrong people. I've seen girls tough it out with their high school friends—accepting a lifestyle they don't like—and use college to get a fresh start and choose the opposite path of their friends.

It saddens me that they'd feel so stuck they're willing to wait it out for years. Yet the fear of being alone (or being left behind) can make anyone play it safe.

God created our daughters to *be* a light and to *live* in the light. They'll always feel the most peace when they lean into this design. Every grade has its own dynamic, and while one class of tenth graders may be wild, the next year's class of tenth graders may have their act together. It's easier for your daughter to be a light when her class dynamic is healthy. It's easier for her to make good choices when that's what many of her classmates do.

> *God created our daughters to be a light and to live in the light. They'll always feel the most peace when they lean into this design.*

Yet in all circumstances, God pursues her heart. He invites her to come closer. Cultivate integrity by teaching your daughter to be a light for her generation. Pray for friends in her circle who aim to do the same.

What Does It Mean to "Be a Light"?

The church was dark, and we were all handed candles as part of a Lenten retreat. The priest lit the first candle from an oil vigil lamp. In the Orthodox church, this lamp—the *kandili*—always burns on the altar table. It symbolizes the eternal light of Christ (John 1).

The kandili reminds us that Jesus is our light and our life. His light illuminates us, guides us, and comforts us. It gives hope and dispels darkness.

Using his candle, the priest lit other candles. One by one we passed the flame around until every candle and face was aglow. I remembered what I once heard: *It takes only one candle to light a thousand others.*

How true that is!

This retreat in Birmingham was led by Father Evan Armatas of Colorado. The theme was "Reclaiming the Great Commission" and living out our call to make disciples of Christ. We spread God's love like we shared the candlelight: one by one with our neighbors, passing on the gift of light. In a healthy church, the room is full of light bearers who strengthen one another and then carry the light of Christ that lives inside them into their everyday lives.

Later that day, Father Evan used these candles again. This time, we lit the candles inside the church—and then walked outside. Father Evan's message was simple: *Take the next step. Don't keep the light to yourself or contain it in a church. Instead, share it with the world. Bring hope into the darkness.*

But the weather didn't cooperate. It was windy, and though people tried to protect their flames by using their hands, many candles blew out. The sound of ambulance sirens downtown and noise in the distance made it hard to concentrate.

When rain began to pour, more flames went out.

Father Evan smiled. "Isn't this representative of life?" he said. "Inside the church, it's easy to spread light. It's easy to feel uplifted and unified. But outside the church walls, we face challenges and resistance. Spreading the light becomes more difficult."

Your daughter should know that being a light is never a perfect process. Some days it feels like two steps forward and three steps back. She needs an inner circle that strengthens her like this church community where we lit one another's candles. Having a secure home base helps her take the brave next step in sharing her light with others.

It's easy to shine light inside a church. But in the real world, your daughter will face some resistance. She'll encounter people or face events that dim her light or test her faith in humanity.

This may look like:

- being joyful and having someone tell her that she is fake;
- planning parties and extending invitations, yet rarely being invited;
- being a good listener, yet longing for someone to listen to her;
- loving the Lord with passion, but being called a Jesus freak;
- writing encouraging notes to her team, but only getting one response;
- sacrificing study time to visit her grandmother, who complains the whole time;
- creating art for a fundraiser, but getting no bids;
- sharing a story about God to a friend who gets mad and leaves;
- enjoying her church friends until she learns that they make fun of her;
- taking the high road with a friend who throws her under the bus; or
- apologizing and forgiving others, yet rarely seeing this reciprocated.

At some point, you've probably experienced resistance too. You know that spreading goodness isn't always rewarding. Some days feel rough. Some days make you want to quit. But you can't go wrong by choosing what is right, and prioritizing integrity trains your daughter to do the right thing even when others don't. It helps her live for God's approval, not human approval (Galatians 1:10), and find peace in that. This peace is priceless. This peace is the prize. You never know who may be influenced by how your daughter lives her life.

Just one candle can light a thousand others. Just one candle can start a domino effect across her generation.

Raise Your Daughter to Notice Others

For many girls today, friendship is a major pain point. The problem is an absence of light.

It's an issue in big cities and small towns too. When a girl feels like nobody sees her or cares, it's just as painful as deliberate meanness. As one girl asked her mom: "What do you do when you feel invisible? How do you make them notice you?"

Sadly, many girls wonder if their life matters. They believe this world would be better without them. Most people would never intentionally make anyone feel invisible, but this is the fallout of a society with a narcissism epidemic.[1]

When we're stuck on ourselves, we fail to see others. Many girls spend hours thinking about the way that people treat them, yet they don't take five minutes to consider how they treat others. They have no idea how many people feel overlooked or forgotten.

If you ask me, *that* is the disconnect. That is why so many girls feel lonely. God created us to be givers, but when we live life as takers—believing the world revolves around us and our needs—relationships become one-sided. They can't grow deep or ever feel truly satisfying.

For this reason, we do our daughters a favor by not treating them like the center of the universe. We empower them to be a light by not worshiping the ground they walk on. We can love them well without encouraging self-absorption or arrogance.

Psychologist and author Dr. Madeline Levine said:

> In order to love healthily, a child cannot believe that the moon and stars revolve around him. Spotlights are blinding, and the child who is constantly told how special he is will have difficulty seeing other people clearly. He is bound to be disappointed when his partner doesn't show the same unbridled enthusiasm his parents once showed for his every effort. I see a steady stream of kids who are profoundly angry and disappointed when their girlfriend or boyfriend dumps them, usually because of their wearisome narcissism.[2]

The good news is, we can prevent this. We can help our daughters look beyond themselves by teaching them to be "balcony girls."

Author Joyce Landorf Heatherley wrote a book called *Balcony People* forty years ago. Her message still rings true today. Balcony people are the loved ones in your life who stand on the balcony to cheer you on. They're encouraging and supportive. They energize you and want you to succeed. When you win, they feel like they've won too.

At the other extreme are basement people. Basement people

tear you down. They're negative and critical, and their voices and evaluations can ring in your head long after they are gone.

God created us to notice and celebrate what is good, right, beautiful, and praiseworthy. He wants us to take a genuine interest in others. If we live correctly, people will miss us when we leave the room. On the day of our funeral, someone will cry and miss us *deeply*.[3]

Your daughter probably knows who her balcony people are. Who makes it easy to be a light? Who lifts her spirits? Who brings out her best?

More importantly, is your daughter a balcony friend? Can she handle a friend's success? What happens when she feels overshadowed or outperformed?

Some girls pretend to stand on the balcony, but their hearts are really in the basement, secretly hoping their friends will fail. A competitive spirit gets in the way.

We all face difficult seasons that make it hard to celebrate. We endure trials that lead us to the basement. But what makes balcony people different, I think, is that balcony people want *out* of the basement. They see jealousy, resentment, and a critical spirit as vices to work on and overcome, not qualities to be proud of.

Girls who become balcony friends naturally attract balcony friends. And the best part is, your daughter can cheer for a girl she barely knows. One simple gesture—like smiling, saying her name, and applauding her talent—could breathe life into a girl who feels invisible. It could affirm that her life matters.

Celebrate your daughter when she's in the spotlight, yet teach her to spotlight others as well. Help her see beyond herself and be a mirror for God's love.

Emphasize Kindness

I often hear from moms who are at their wit's end trying to create a kinder dynamic at their daughter's school.

Especially in places known for academic excellence (Christian schools included), competition can trump kindness. The "win at all costs" mentality can undermine friendships.

Either at school or another venue, your daughter will encounter competitive people who make it hard to be kind. She may lose confidence, shut down, or feel isolated because she's not sure who to trust.

What used to be common sense isn't common anymore. When my friend led a Bible study for high schoolers and talked about choosing kind words, they flatly told her, "That sounds weird. Nobody talks like that." Sadly, we live in an age where encouraging words and social graces feel foreign to many people— and it's okay to be mean if you make people laugh.

What often happens, temporarily, is that kind girls fall through the cracks. In preschool and early grade school, they're usually well liked, but as middle school approaches, the social hierarchy shifts. Kindness isn't always cool, and being left out or forgotten makes many kind girls wonder what is wrong with them.

Especially in middle school, the girls who often attract the most attention—or hold the most power—are domineering or mean. Since their classmates don't have the maturity yet to know what to do, they let the alpha dogs run the show.

Yet here's what happens as everyone grows up: Many girls will decide that kindness is the top quality they want in a friend. Many girls will be burned by mean friends—and decide to never go back. They'll feel *determined* to make better choices.

So while kindness may not make your daughter the queen bee

of middle school or the rock star of high school, it does set her up to thrive long term. It keeps her at peace with herself and God. It leads to genuine, lifelong friendships.

And while mean girls will still exist beyond high school, girls who choose this path will reap what they sow. They'll face the consequences of hurtful behavior as they lose friends, make the wrong person mad, meet their match in someone meaner than them, or miss out on an opportunity (like a job they want or a guy they like) because their mean reputation preceded them.

Mean girls will also struggle to find peace. God can't bless a path of self-destruction, and this is why we pray for hearts to soften to let Him in.

If your daughter is trying to be a light yet is falling through the cracks, show her extra love. Get her plugged into a meaningful group (like Young Life, a nonprofit, or a ministry where she leads younger girls) that appreciates and welcomes her bright personality. These connections can be a saving grace. They can offer a place of belonging for your daughter if she's floating between friend groups and not receiving invitations.

> *God can't bless a path of self-destruction, and this is why we pray for hearts to soften to let Him in.*

I meet a lot of kind girls who "floated" in high school yet thrived as they left home. Getting a fresh start in a bigger sea helped them find similar friends, friends who could appreciate their loving heart and kindness.

But watching your daughter struggle in that messy middle place can be very emotional. Nobody likes to see their child upset. Nobody enjoys rejection. My best advice is to take the high road when you can and don't be impulsive, especially if Mama Bear gets triggered. I realize this isn't easy, but what's happening more and more these days is that moms are ending *their* friendships over their daughters' social lives. Moms are demanding confrontations that don't solve the problem.

The scenario often goes like this: Two moms have been friends forever. They've raised their girls together (let's call them Jane and Sarah) and vacationed together as families. The situation is ideal until Sarah pulls away in middle school. Jane is upset—and her mom is livid. She can't believe her friend would let Sarah treat her daughter this way. Even if Jane finds new friends, her mom can't let it go. She ends her friendship with the other mom and wonders if it was real.

On one hand, I get it. I've been on both sides of the parting scenario, and the urge to find closure is real. Sometimes distance is necessary when the pain runs deep. Sometimes moms should get involved when mediation is needed.

But young friendships can be fluid, and they aren't always set in stone. When we act prematurely, we do things we'll regret. We fail to model temperance by acting on our emotions.

And here's the bigger truth: Old friends often reunite. Girls often circle back to friendships that were real. Our kids can be very forgiving, and they may work through their issues over time.

Where does that leave you—and the mom friendship you canceled—if your daughter and her daughter reunite? Wouldn't you wish that you'd waited to see how the story played out?

When my daughter and her childhood bestie suddenly parted ways, it broke my heart. I loved this girl, and I dreamed of them being college roommates and lifelong friends.

But in middle school, they drifted apart. They stopped speaking and had nothing in common. I wanted to force them back together, but I knew that wasn't right. I also debated how to handle my friendship with her mom. Should we stop talking too?

Luckily, she kept being kind to me, so I did the same. We didn't burn that bridge. This is when I learned to keep my mom friendships separate from my kids' friendships—to not let my social life depend on theirs. While this mom and I weren't as close as we'd been before, we did remain friendly. We chatted when we saw each other.

Six years later, our girls reconnected. They became close again, and we took a senior trip together. When the other mom told me, "I'm so happy our girls reunited!" I told her, "Me too. And the best part is, we had nothing to do with it. They did this on their own."

My dream of a lifelong friendship may happen after all, but if I'd come unhinged, I may have burned that bridge. I may have taught my daughter to burn that bridge too.

You can't control your daughter's friendships. You can't presume to know what happens in someone else's home. Your friend may be coaching her daughter well—yet her daughter won't listen. Maybe she resists her mom's lessons on being kind, and since your friend's loyalty is with her family, she can't share the full story. She can only take her struggle to God.

Kindness isn't weakness—and it doesn't mean being a doormat. It doesn't mean that you or your daughter shouldn't set healthy boundaries with hurtful people. It's possible to be kind *and* strong. Honest *and* tactful. Friendly in making small talk *and* careful in knowing who to trust.

Many girls regret being mean, but few regret being kind. While kindness may seem counterintuitive in an alpha dog world, it will help your daughter feel proud of the person she is becoming. It will allow her to thrive without selling out.

Pray for Light to Find Light

One of my favorite parts of signing books is meeting bright-eyed teenage girls. Sometimes their radiance is so palpable that I can't help but say, "That light in your eyes is amazing. Always protect it, and don't let anyone steal it."

Because life has a way of extinguishing the light our daughters are meant to shine. Challenging people and experiences can crush their spirit. They need friends who help protect their light. Loved ones who keep it alive and rekindle it when needed.

As my girls navigate life, I pray for light to find light. I pray for friends who live with integrity. Other parents are praying similar prayers, and when the time is right, our children will meet.

Several years ago, I met an adorable mom named Caroline after an event I had in Georgia. Our daughters had grown close as Big Sister / Little Sister in their Auburn University sorority, and we wanted to meet too. When Caroline told me, "It's a great feeling when your child benefits from someone else's parenting," I assured her that feeling was mutual. The blessing feels bigger on my end.

Just weeks earlier, my friend Marci had shown me a picture that her son sent her via text while visiting Caroline's family lake home. Their sons are roommates at Auburn, and Marci's son sent her a picture of a sign in this home that read:

Our Family Rules

Pray often (always).
Find your identity in Christ.
Show the same grace to others that God shows you.
Encourage others. Love others.

Be kind.

Listen—no yelling or elbowing.

Be first to say sorry.

Slow dance in the kitchen.

Always be looking for ways to serve others.

Be thankful.

Fill the house with music. Worship.

Hug one another (daily).

"Consider it pure joy . . . when you face trials." (James 1:2)

The sign reminded him of his mom (Marci) and what she'd taught him. Two boys raised with similar values crossed paths in college, and in that big sea of people, they gravitated to what felt familiar.

Again and again, I've seen this dynamic happen. I've watched children raised with similar values organically find one another. *Water seeks its own level, and when your daughter lives with integrity, she'll attract friends who do the same. She'll find friends who make her better.*

Your daughter may face a social shake-up or two before she finishes high school. She may drift apart from old friends or learn lessons about bad company (1 Corinthians 15:33). Don't fear a lonely season that may give her the reset she needs. Don't discount what God can do even when her heart is broken.

Instead, pray for light to find light. Remind her to wish the best for her friends even if they part ways. People can significantly change with time and maturity. Old friends can become close again. Acquaintances can become loyal allies. God will constantly weave different life stories together, so help your daughter choose the best path without burning bridges she may regret.

Packing integrity in your daughter's suitcase is essential because without it, she'll drift. She'll lose her way and her moral compass. You can't force your daughter to show integrity—or assume she's set for life if she shows integrity now—but you can point her toward people and places that inspire her best. God wants what is good for your daughter more than you want it for her, so pray for His will. Pray for the magnification and preservation of the light that lives inside her.

Truths Worth Packing

- "You are the light of the world—like a city on a hilltop that cannot be hidden. No one lights a lamp and then puts it under a basket. Instead, a lamp is placed on a stand, where it gives light to everyone in the house. In the same way, let your good deeds shine out for all to see, so that everyone will praise your heavenly Father." (Matthew 5:14–16)
- "Jesus spoke to the people once more and said, 'I am the light of the world. If you follow me, you won't have to walk in darkness, because you will have the light that leads to life.'" (John 8:12)
- "Point your kids in the right direction—when they're old they won't be lost." (Proverbs 22:6 MSG)
- "As iron sharpens iron, so one person sharpens another." (Proverbs 27:17 NIV)

- "So encourage each other and build each other up, just as you are already doing." (1 Thessalonians 5:11)

Questions to Unpack

1. Has your daughter ever experienced an unhealthy friend group? Have you ever encouraged her to stay for the wrong reasons? If so, what happened?
2. Which environments or people bring out your daughter's best? What has dimmed her light, dampened her faith, or kept her from being a balcony girl?
3. Name a time when someone's child benefitted from your parenting. What lesson, habit, or value did you instill that helped your daughter be a light? How did it make her feel to have this positive impact?

A Prayer to Lighten Your Load

Dear Lord,
Let light find light. Connect my daughter with friends who reflect Your love. When she faces a lonely spell, put a song in her heart. Fill the void inside her with a deeper love for You. I praise You for the light of Christ that keeps hope alive. Give me wisdom as I guide my daughter and trust what You have planned. In Jesus' name, amen.

CHAPTER 4

RELATIONSHIP SMARTS

MODEL HEALTHY RELATIONSHIPS

*You should choose people who want things to be
better, not worse. It's a good thing, not a selfish
thing, to choose people who are good for you.*

JORDAN PETERSON

It was an argument that broke my heart—and scared me for
the girl.

My husband and I had just attended a nighttime college football game. As we walked out of the stadium with ninety thousand
other fans, we heard vulgarities and cursing in front of us. A couple
in their late twenties appeared to be having a lovers' quarrel.

The guy looked like a bodybuilder. His face was red with rage
as he yelled. The girl was petite and half his size. She was screaming at him and dishing it back.

My husband stopped me to create distance between us and this couple. Spectators watched with horror as the guy's anger amplified; several men looked ready to spring into action if he lost control and lashed out.

The girl yelled at the guy and then walked off. *Keep going,* I thought. *You don't need him or this relationship. If he treats you like this in public, there's no telling what he does in private.*

She walked alone for about twenty seconds, but then she turned around and went back to him. I watched with disbelief as this couple walked off together in silence, neither of them saying a word. I felt sick to my stomach wondering and worrying about what might happen when they got home.

It broke my heart that anyone would stay in a relationship this toxic. It pained me to witness this because I have four daughters, and the thought of them being in an abusive relationship is one of my deepest fears.

Because the truth is, bad relationships don't start off rough. In most cases, they feel magical. They seem too good to be true, and with time you learn they are.

Just because a girl is raised in a loving home doesn't mean that she's protected. Even girls with great upbringings can be susceptible to bad relationships for reasons like these:

- They're often very trusting, as they haven't witnessed firsthand how bad some people can be.
- They're more likely to be compassionate and empathetic, sometimes loyal to a fault.
- They don't give up easily on people or relationships.
- They may be quick to forgive and give second chances.
- They've been taught to love everyone, yet they don't

understand the need for discernment and setting healthy boundaries.

In the real world, some people are very manipulative. Some people call themselves Christians—yet their behavior tells a different story. Even girls with great role models may need extra coaching in learning how to spot a fake.

When you've grown up surrounded by trustworthy people, you assume that most people are trustworthy. You're not always as savvy or street smart as someone who's been exposed to dark situations.

Thankfully, God gives our daughters (and us) the gift of discernment. He uses the Holy Spirit to guide us, nudge us, and help us judge relationships. Things like gut instincts, intuition, red flags, epiphanies, a lack of peace, or a sudden sense that something isn't right are ways that He speaks to us. Whether we ignore these clues or pay attention makes a difference in the relationships we choose.

Nothing will get your daughter off track faster than a bad influence or a misguided quest for love. The company she keeps sets the trajectory for her future, and even smart girls can make bad decisions when their hearts get involved. Even girls who normally make good choices can wind up in trouble. Your daughter may not see the red flags or understand why character matters until the consequences play out.

Helping her build healthy relationships is a cornerstone of her well-being. It is time well spent with her. As the old saying goes, "Show me your friends, and I'll show you your future." The older your daughter gets, the more influence her friends and boyfriends will have.

She needs your positive example to see how healthy relationships work. She'll learn more from your example than your advice.

She also needs discernment—the ability to judge new situations and people well—as she encounters new experiences. Teach your daughter what it means to have the *heart* of a child and the *mind* of an adult.[1] Encourage healthy choices as she relies on these two things to develop her relationship smarts.

What Was Modeled for You— or Not Modeled?

I feel fortunate that I grew up in a healthy home. My parents got the big things right. They cultivated faith, confidence, and a sense of purpose. They loved me and my siblings well.

I was born in the seventies and grew up in the eighties. The parenting advice, according to my mom, was to be "hands-off." Apparently, the parents before her generation had been very hands-on, and some experts speculated that their overzealousness made their kids rebel and become hippies.

Hoping to avoid that, my mom's generation swung the other way. They parented differently, and maybe this explains why the parents of Generation X kids gave us a lot of autonomy. In some ways, we raised ourselves. We learned to be independent and figure things out.

I had a solid childhood, but one skill I never learned was conflict resolution. Back then, intentional parenting wasn't a trend, so we did things our way. As the fourth child in a family of five kids, I had to be scrappy. I learned early how to hold my own and not get pushed around.

When my sisters and I argued, usually over clothes, we never apologized. We didn't say, "I'm sorry" or admit our mistakes. Instead, we just didn't speak for three days. We avoided one another until we cooled down, and once we talked again, the fight was assumed to be over. We acted as if it never happened.

I didn't question this habit until I brought it into *my* family. As my oldest daughter became a teenager and we began to argue, teenage Kari came out. A side of me that I thought I'd buried was really lying dormant, and in the heat of the moment, she came back to life.

Arguing but never apologizing created a gulf between me and my daughter. If I didn't find a new approach, I knew that gap would grow. My pride would come between us.

This revelation inspired *Love Her Well*, my first book for moms. Helping mothers and daughters connect has been deeply rewarding, and what I now understand is that nobody enters motherhood with every skill they need. Nobody comes without baggage or a generational pattern that needs to be broken. Nobody's parents covered *every* base in preparing them for life.

We all lack some essential skills that nobody packed in our suitcase. We've all heard advice as adults that we wish we'd learned as a child.

Before we collectively blame our parents (or send them our therapy bills), let's remember that no parent is perfect. Every parent begins their journey a little bit clueless. Just as we hope our kids will show *us* grace as they reflect on their childhood, our parents need grace too. Most parents do the best they can with what they know at the time. Most parents wish they could go back in time and do a few things differently.

Thankfully, it's never too late to add new skills to your own suitcase. You don't have to be a perfect parent to raise a daughter who is ready for life. As you raise her, God raises you. Even if you're struggling to get to a better place, you can be a great role model. You can show your daughter what it means to be a human in a broken world.

You don't have to be a perfect parent to raise a daughter who is ready for life.

You can only take your daughter as far as you have come, and rather than feel defeated by what your suitcase lacks, let her see you add new essentials. Whether it's a new skill, perspective, strategy, or way to evaluate relation-ships, she benefits from seeing your suitcase as a lifelong work in progress.

Because guess what? Her suitcase is a work in progress too. It will keep evolving and growing as she grows up.

Our girls are very intuitive. They notice how we treat others, and how we let others treat us. Model in your life what your daughter deserves in her life. Show self-compassion as you learn the life skills you wish you'd known all along.

Teach Your Daughter to Trust Her Gut

My daughter and I visited Nashville for a fun weekend together before she left home. At a trendy downtown restaurant, the wait-ress seated us next to the entertainment, a young musician whose father was playing back-up guitar.

During their break, we talked to them. This father of five had flown in to support his son, and when he heard that my daughter was headed to college, he looked her straight in the eye and said, "I tell my daughters: You better be as smart as you are pretty. Book smart, street smart, and emotionally intelligent . . . because the devil always has a counterfeit." I was thankful for his wisdom that reinforced what we taught at home. I hoped my daughter would take it to heart.

Like me, this father has parented for more than two decades. We've both seen a lot transpire, and it's led us to conclusions like this: Our daughters are smart—smarter than us at their age—but their life experience is limited. They can be naive and gullible, and they're still growing their spirit of discernment. They can't always tell the difference between the weeds and the wheat (Matthew 13:24–30).

While some girls have a strong sixth sense, other girls don't. They need reminders to listen to their gut. Here's a story that helps explain why: I once called a friend to warn her about her daughter's new boyfriend. I'd never made a call like this, but given the strong evidence that I knew, I felt led to speak up.

Another friend's daughter had recently dated this boy, and he proved to be a sweet-talking narcissist. He'd given that girlfriend a sob story that his bad boy reputation was no longer true, and she believed him until his entire baseball team urged her to break up with him.

At practice this boy kept bragging about the lewd plans he had for his girlfriend if she didn't cooperate. It turned out he hadn't changed at all. He'd also been suspended from school for soliciting nude photos from multiple girls.

His new girlfriend was in a different grade, and she didn't know his history. I shared the facts with my friend and asked her not to mention my name. She was thankful that I called and passed the information on to her daughter.

At first, her daughter was shocked. "I just don't see it," she told her mom. "He's so sweet to me."

Her mom told her to think about it and pray about it too. Her daughter had a busy week of practices that didn't allow much time with this boy.

Three days later, she broke up with him. She made this decision alone, without external pressure or input. After taking some time to reflect, she recalled moments that gave her pause. There were clues that seemed a little off, but she'd dismissed them because she liked this boy. He acted exceptionally nice to her.

Many of us have made this mistake with people who seem "nice." We've ignored our instincts, talked ourselves out of our feelings, or felt guilty for being skeptical.

But charm can be deceptive (Proverbs 31:30), and getting weird vibes, funny feelings, or stirrings of unrest are worth taking time to examine. God may be telling us to guard our heart and not dive into that relationship.

It's common for girls to put a boy (or a friend) on a pedestal they don't deserve to be on. This infatuation can quickly blind them to the unvarnished truth. But people are meant to be loved, not worshiped. Only God deserves to be on a pedestal, and when we don't worship Him, we find a substitute. We make an idol of a person or a thing that becomes the center of our universe.

While I don't have a foolproof plan to save your daughter from bad relationships, I can offer these guidelines to help her choose good company:

- Healthy relationships inspire the best version of you. Unhealthy relationships bring out your worst. *(Like this chapter's opening story.)*
- Healthy relationships draw you closer to the people who love you most, like your family and lifelong friends. Unhealthy

relationships isolate you and create division in your closest relationships. *(Good friends bring harmony into your home. They're kind to your parents, your siblings, and you. A narcissist, on the other hand, will slowly cut you off from your support system so you only listen to them. In marriage this can look like moving you far away from home or not giving you a car in order to limit your independence.)*

- Healthy relationships are a major source of comfort. Unhealthy relationships are a major source of stress. *(Good people offer an escape from life's harsh realities. They energize you rather than drain you.)*

- Healthy relationships build your confidence. Unhealthy relationships destroy it. *(When someone is more critical of you than you are of yourself, that's a red flag. Distance yourself before you start trusting their opinion over your own.)*

- Healthy relationships enrich your life. You won't regret them in the end. Unhealthy relationships wreck your future, leaving you to deal with the ruins. *(As Andy Stanley said, "Don't trade your future for someone who won't be there in the future!"[2] Be smart up front.)*

- Healthy relationships lead you to good places. Unhealthy relationships don't. *(Nashville counselor David Thomas recalled a sixteen-year-old boy who concluded, after many dead-end relationships, that he was looking in all the wrong places. He finally realized, "I've got a better chance of meeting a great girl at Young Life than I do at a party with marijuana."[3])*

- Healthy relationships keep you on track. Unhealthy relationships let you self-destruct. *(Love wants what is best for a person long-term. And real friends will upset you if that's what it takes to save you. As Dr. Tim Keller said, "Like a surgeon, true friends only cut you in order to heal you."[4])*

- Healthy relationships bring peace. Unhealthy relationships bring unrest. *(A clear conscience is the softest pillow. It lets you sleep well at night. Don't make a mistake like the college freshman girl who joined a mean friend group—and then broke down in tears one night while yelling at a girl as she finally admitted, "I hate how mean I've become. I hate acting this way to fit in with my friends." That tension was God at work in her heart, calling her to a better way.)*

Again, bad relationships don't start off rough. At first, they feel magical.

Remind your daughter to check someone's character before falling for their charisma. Just as the quality of a tree can be identified by the fruit it produces (Matthew 12:33), what plays out in someone's life shows the condition of their heart. Do they bring peace . . . or havoc? Joy . . . or cynicism? Faithfulness . . . or infidelity? Hope . . . or negativity? What do people with firsthand knowledge of that person say?

Virtues like love, joy, peace, patience, kindness, goodness, faithfulness, gentleness, and self-control are fruit of the Holy Spirit (Galatians 5:22–23). They manifest when someone has Jesus in their heart. Anyone who shows the opposite traits isn't a great candidate to build a life with, not unless they take steps to change.

People tend to get more pronounced with age, and little problems can snowball into big problems when they go unaddressed.

A little anger problem at age twenty can look like rage at age fifty.

A little drinking problem can become alcoholism.

A little negativity can later look like constant criticism.

And a little spending problem can turn into debt.

When people share their cautionary tales about a bad relationship, they often admit that the warning signs were there, but at first they seemed insignificant. Only in hindsight can they see the rumblings of a future storm.

I once met a dad who told his daughters, "If a boy ever tries to come between you and God, he wasn't sent by God." This is true in friendships too. The best people will always draw your daughter closer to the Lord. They'll bring an overwhelming sense of peace.

Remind Your Daughter to Cast a Wide Net

Making healthy relationship choices is easier when your daughter has options.

She can grow her options by casting a wide net. I tell my girls: "Cast a wide net by being kind to everyone. Make new friends wherever you go. It's okay to have your best friends, but don't let that keep you from making new friends too."

I knew the message had resonated when my daughters started to tell me, "She's my friend from French class," "She's my friend from PE," or "She's my friend from tumbling." Casting a wide net didn't feel natural at first, but with practice they got better. They stretched beyond their comfort zones and discovered the joy of broader connections.

Many girls paint themselves into a corner by never branching out. When drama blows up their friend group, they have nowhere to go. Nobody invites them in because they acted so exclusive.

But if your daughter has cast a wide net, she'll have other

options. She won't be stuck or left alone if her closest friends suddenly turn on her.

This happened to one of my daughters in the eighth grade. Her best friends shut her out during a weekend retreat, and she wasn't allowed to sit, talk, or interact with them.

As you'd imagine, she was crushed, but thankfully she'd been friendly beyond her friend group. She'd learned to branch out that year. Guess who swooped in to save the day? Guess who let her join them and saved her from sitting alone?

Her other friends. The new connections she'd recently made. On a hard day of her young life, casting a wide net paid off, and I was glad I'd taught her this lesson.

I could also see God's hand in this lesson. As much as it pained me to see her upset, I knew that she needed this experience to understand why kindness matters. When her friends tried to isolate another girl six months later, she refused to participate. God used her pain for good to make her a kinder person.

Casting a wide net improves your daughter's odds of finding friends she can trust. Many girls stay stuck in trusting the wrong people. They let their boyfriend or their friends continually hurt them and give everyone equal access to their private life.

Remind your daughter that trust isn't earned over a week, a spring break trip, or one semester of school. Trust isn't given freely to everyone, regardless of their motives or intentions. Instead, trust builds over time. Trust will come as your daughter observes a person's choices, character, and behavior.

While she is called to love everyone, not everyone deserves a place in her innermost circle. Some people can be loved up close and personal—and others are best loved at an arm's distance. Your daughter can be friendly without sharing her secrets. She can stick to small talk with her weekday friends and go deeper with her weekend friends.

The company she chooses will profoundly impact the life that she will have. She will date (and marry) to her level of health. So help your daughter address her own blind spots and weaknesses. Model what is healthy and right. As author Robert Fulghum said, "Don't worry that [your children] never listen to you; worry that they are always watching you."[5] When you build healthy relationships, you inspire your child to do the same.

People will enter your daughter's life for a reason, a season, or a lifetime. Even short relationships can serve a purpose by confirming what she does or doesn't want. Every experience grows her social intelligence, and the worst-behaving people offer the best example of how *not* to act. They help your daughter learn how to guard her heart, set boundaries, and decide who she can trust.

Packing relationship smarts in your daughter's suitcase is essential because it helps her make good judgment calls. It teaches her how to gauge new people and new environments. Pray for unhealthy relationships to last for a season and for healthy relationships to last for a lifetime. Pray for her to trust her gut wherever her journey takes her.

Truths Worth Packing

- "Look, I am sending you out as sheep among wolves. So be as shrewd as snakes and harmless as doves." (Matthew 10:16)

- "Don't just pretend to love others. Really love them. Hate what is wrong. Hold tightly to what is good." (Romans 12:9)
- "Here's what I want: Give me a God-listening heart so I can lead your people well, discerning the difference between good and evil. For who on their own is capable of leading your glorious people?" (1 Kings 3:9 MSG)
- "Follow my example, as I follow the example of Christ." (1 Corinthians 11:1 NIV)
- "Guard your heart above all else, for it determines the course of your life." (Proverbs 4:23)

Questions to Unpack

1. On a scale of 1 to 10, how adept is your daughter in choosing healthy relationships (with 1 being not very adept and 10 being very adept)? Where does she have room to grow?
2. Have you ever shared a personal story about failing to see or tune into a relationship red flag? What example can you give your daughter to help her learn from your mistake?
3. Do you believe a bad relationship can grow your daughter's social intelligence? What are the takeaways from these situations?

A Prayer to Lighten Your Load

Dear Lord,

Bless my daughter's relationships. Create chemistry with positive people and give her the courage to walk away when something isn't right. I praise You for the intuition that guides and protects my daughter. Let her closest relationships inspire a deeper love for You and bring out her best. In Jesus' name, amen.

CHAPTER 5

PERSPECTIVE

CULTIVATE A POSITIVE OUTLOOK

When I realized I was more obsessed
with what was broken than with what
was beautiful, I made some changes.

REBEKAH LYONS

My husband tried to hug me, but I shook him off. I wasn't in the mood to be hugged, and it bothered me that he tried.

My reaction had nothing to do with him. I love Harry, and I'm thankful that he's affectionate.

But ten seconds before he walked into the bedroom, a post on social media got under my skin. I was ruminating on that post when he tried to hug me.

A stranger I don't know wrote a message I can't remember—but what I *can* remember is letting that message ruin this moment with my better half.

Poor Harry was just saying good morning. He was enjoying

IS YOUR DAUGHTER READY?

our spring break vacation, and I'd enjoyed this family trip, too, until a quick scroll through my news feed suddenly flipped my mood.

In a matter of seconds, my heart went from soft and relaxed to combative and tense. It turned me into the person I *don't* like to be—the mom version of Dr. Jekyll and Mr. Hyde.

I blamed myself for letting my perspective be so easily tampered with. I set my phone down so that external forces wouldn't steal my joy or my ability to love my family.

After all, my family is my heart. I don't want to waste our limited time together, especially on vacation. Twenty years from now, when they remember me in this season, I want them to picture me with a smile on my face, not a scowl.

A few weeks later, I shared my story with a friend. She nodded and described a similar experience, saying, "Oh yes. My friend made me feel bad—and my family suffered the consequences."

Isn't this the truth? Do you ever find yourself here as well? We live in an age of hair-trigger reactions, and the people we hurt the most are often the people we love the most. Emotions like frustration, anger, fear, or pain can roll out like a chain reaction. If we don't check ourselves, we'll wreck ourselves—and quickly lose sight of reality.

It reminds me of the saying: *The boss yells at the man. The man yells at his wife. The wife yells at the kid. And the kid kicks the dog.* Until we break the cycle, we pass our feelings on. We either internalize what triggers us or dump it on others.

Neither option is healthy.

Neither option makes anyone happy.

Neither option helps us raise confident girls who can give themselves a reality check when their perspective gets tampered with. Our children deserve better, and as moms, we lead the charge in teaching them better. We shape their worldview and perspective.

So many teenage girls I know remind me of their mothers. From their witty jokes to their good manners to their ability to laugh at themselves, I know *exactly* who shaped their positive outlook. I see what they've picked up by exposure and osmosis.

These girls are always mature for their age, and they start life with a big leg up through the extension of their mother's wisdom.

I've also seen many girls (mine included) treat minor issues like major emergencies. My daughter, for instance, once called me in tears. She was sobbing so hard she couldn't talk, and I honestly thought that someone had died. I panicked and left the gym to walk outside and hear her. When she finally caught her breath, she shared what happened.

Thankfully, there was no tragic event. She'd just experienced a female rite of passage: She absolutely hated her new haircut. The stylist cut it too short, and she had a party the next day that she no longer wanted to go to.

This overreaction wasn't typical for her, and now wasn't the time to tell my daughter to just chill and calm down. She needed a little empathy and reassurance that she looked beautiful. In my mind, however, I realized how we had some perspective work to do. I remembered myself at her age, crying over a haircut that I hated too. I guess the apple doesn't fall far from the tree.

Like my daughters, I've treated minor issues like major emergencies.

I've let worry steal my peace.

I've fixated on issues that won't matter in six months.

I've had overblown reactions I regretted.

I've let jealousy consume me.

I've chosen grumbling over gratitude.

I've lost sight of my blessings as I compared myself to others.

I've fought the wrong battles—and had no energy left for the battles that matter most.

And I've dwelled on what is *wrong* rather than celebrated what is *right*.

We can't control the world, but we can control our interpretation of it. We can ask God to renew our minds with a healthy outlook that we can model for our daughters.

> *We can't control the world, but we can control our interpretation of it.*

Perspective repaints the big picture. It offers a lens of hope. It helps us get our thinking straight.

David Thomas described perspective as learning to accurately categorize life events: understanding that on a scale of 1 to 10, losing your car keys is a 1, while losing a family member is a 10. Perspective, he said, is like the pain scale used by doctors. When you can accurately describe your pain, they can appropriately treat your pain. Without perspective, kids go off the rails over insignificant events. More than ever, kids are swinging to a 10 for any life event. They can't properly assign the significance of their experience on a scale.[1]

We can't expect more from our daughters than we do from ourselves. Teaching them to appropriately scale an experience starts with our example. We've all been guilty of getting so immersed in the weeds of life that we microscopically focus on today. We lose sight of the big picture.

When my mental framework feels faulty, I know that it's time to breathe, pull back, and see the aerial view. It's time to look at life through the lens of eternity. Next to a magnificent God, today's problems and glitches suddenly look small. Current circumstances feel more bearable. As we fix our eyes on heaven, we receive the gift of clearer vision. We can feel hopeful for what's to come through a healthy, life-giving outlook—and teach our daughters to do the same.

What Mental Pivots Do You Make?

We can't choose what challenges we face in life. But we can choose our perspective, attitude, and mindset. We can decide what outlook we bring to the table.

On the day my friend Lori became a mom, she experienced extreme emotions. On one hand, she felt euphoria when meeting her son. On the other hand, she felt the heartache of learning that he was born deaf.

The doctor's delivery of the news wasn't ideal, and Lori felt overwhelmed. But when her pediatrician came the very next day, her perspective did a one-eighty.

"This is life-*changing*, Lori, but it's not life-*threatening*," the pediatrician told her. "We can handle this. We'll get through it."

From that moment on, Lori felt capable. She felt extra purpose as a mom, a determination to make sure that her son always felt loved and supported.

Today, he is sixteen and thriving. He enjoys full hearing through a hidden hearing aid, thanks to advances in technology. He loves music and even took piano lessons at age seven. In middle school, he played in the band, and now he serves on the tech crew for high school musicals. Of all their family members, he received the musical talent. God has blessed him with that gift.

Lori says, "Things don't always go according to your plan, but there is *a* plan. You won't be abandoned."

Another friend of mine is walking through a nightmare in her marriage. Her husband is battling addiction, and for years they've faced a pending divorce.

When we last spoke, she spent an hour telling me about God's faithfulness. She had countless stories about the ways He's protected her and surrounded her with the right people. She's much stronger today than even a year ago, and while her heart is still broken, she's never felt closer to God. He hasn't left her for one second.

Corrie ten Boom, in her autobiography *The Hiding Place*, also offered tremendous perspective describing life in a German concentration camp.

Corrie and her sister, Betsie, snuck a Bible into the camp. At night they'd secretly read it with other prisoners. Betsie taught Corrie to seize every opportunity to minister, even in tragic circumstances. Betsie gave thanks in all circumstances (1 Thessalonians 5:18), and Corrie felt sure that her sister had lost her mind when she even gave thanks for the fleas that infested their room in a new barracks assignment.

Who on earth would do that?

But in this new room, the prisoners had more freedom. They could pray and worship for hours with almost no supervision.

Corrie had always believed the Bible, yet her experience in a concentration camp took her faith beyond belief. She wrote, "It was simply a description of the way things were—of hell and heaven, of how men act and how God acts." In one of the darkest corners on earth, the Bible felt like a blazing fire, drawing in prisoners with its warmth and light. Betsie later learned why the guards rarely visited this room: The fleas kept them away. Corrie then remembered her sister giving thanks to God for creatures she saw no use for.[2]

Clearly, these are all examples of big perspective shifts. Sometimes a big mental shift is needed, especially in a crisis. Typically, however, we need smaller mental pivots. We need help reframing the highs and lows of everyday life.

More than ever before, girls are struggling with perspective. They face a mental health epidemic that has sent anxiety rates skyrocketing.

Even before the global pandemic, this was happening:

- Teen girl suicide rates hit a forty-year high; from 2007 to 2015, rates more than doubled.
- Teen depression and anxiety rates jumped 70 percent in twenty years.
- American teens and young adults had much higher depression rates than their counterparts who lived during the Great Depression, World War II, and the Vietnam War. This increased anxiety didn't seem connected to real dangers. It didn't correspond with events that traditionally affected mental health (such as wars, poverty, famine, and security threats). Instead, this "rise seems to have much more to do with the way young people experience the world."[3]

In other words, the way our children interpret life and scale their experiences deeply impacts their mental health. Catastrophic thinking can lead to negative thought loops and higher anxiety.

Counselor Sissy Goff described anxiety as an overestimation of the problem and an underestimation of ourselves. Even as grown-ups, we often don't believe we're capable. The girls in our lives don't believe they're capable either.[4]

Anxiety breeds fear. It blows events out of proportion and can lead us to rescue our kids rather than teach them how to cope, face challenges, and tap into their inner resilience.

Anxious parents are *seven times more likely* to have anxious kids.[5] Personally, this motivates me. It inspires me to improve my mental health so I don't pass down my baggage.

A counselor once told me that if we don't put our anxiety into something bigger and higher than ourselves, we'll micromanage it. This, I believe, is where we get tripped up as moms. This is where we spiral and assume the future depends solely on *us*. This is where we can panic and try to control things as the weight of the world falls on our shoulders. We imagine the future without Jesus—and forget that God gives us the grace to handle whatever comes our way. He opens doors that need to be opened.

My daughter really needed this specific reminder one night. On top of a rigorous junior year course load, she was stressed about the ACT. She'd taken it multiple times, but her progress was minimal. Standardized tests aren't her thing, and despite a high GPA, she worried that she wouldn't get into her first-choice college.

Honestly, I felt worried too. I considered doubling down on ACT tutors. I racked my brain for ways to get her score up. I'm a doer by nature, so taking extra action is often my first response.

But when my daughter broke down into tears that night, my husband and I took the pressure off. We told her, "God has a great plan for your life, and you're working hard and doing your part. If things don't go the way you hope, He'll create a new path. He'll open doors that need to be opened. We're not worried, and we don't want you to worry either. You'll go to college somewhere, and things will work out. Take that pressure off yourself."

Immediately, we saw visible relief on her face. It felt so good to *lighten* her load rather than *add* more stress by telling her to do more, be more, and try harder.

To say this, however, I had to mean it. I had to truly trust God and not cave to my fear that she wouldn't get in. Ironically, she did get into her first-choice college—and then she chose another university! I was so glad that I didn't let my anxiety make her already stressful junior year completely miserable.

Nothing is worth the sacrifice of our daughters' mental health. No success will matter if their inner struggles overwhelm their joy.

Another daughter of mine experienced a panic attack in eighth grade. She froze while taking a test, and when the class ended and her teacher said that time was up, she burst into tears. She couldn't speak for twenty minutes.

She'd never had a panic attack before, so this was unexpected. Just the night before, she'd felt tremendous peace as she thanked God for her blessings. She felt like she was in a great place after two years of being hard on herself.

Thankfully, her teacher was an angel. She spent twenty minutes comforting my daughter and shared a personal story about a struggle from her childhood. When my daughter jumped in my car that afternoon and told me what happened, she wasn't embarrassed or scared that she might have a panic attack again. She knew she could handle it, and it made me proud to see her maturity, self-awareness, and understanding that God was with her even when she couldn't talk.

The next day, we had her fourteen-year-old checkup. When we told her pediatrician what happened, the pediatrician said that what she sees in healthy kids is that their body knows where it feels "safe" to break down. Stress you don't know you are carrying may suddenly come out.

Had my daughter been with a different teacher, a teacher without compassion, she might have held her stress in for self-preservation. The ability to differentiate where it feels safe to fall apart is actually a sign of health. My daughter was right on track.

In her book *Try Softer*, Aundi Kolber says, "I didn't realize then that our wounds often surface only when at last we feel physically or emotionally safe. Once we are out of survival mode, our bodies, minds, and spirits can finally bear to consider our stories and the reasons we are so emotionally dysregulated."[6]

Having perspective isn't about making life perfect; it's about keeping a healthy outlook when life is imperfect. We all face challenges. We all need safe places to feel sad and fall apart. We all need permission to feel our messy emotions and people who bring us to a place of peace. Most of all, we all need God to comfort us, enlighten us, and lead us.

> *We all need permission to feel our messy emotions and people who bring us to a place of peace.*

Remind your daughter that she can do hard things. Help her reframe her tough situations. When she is weak, God is strong. His power is made perfect in weakness (2 Corinthians 12:8–10).

Reframing can look like this:

- Yes, school may be harder for your daughter because she has dyslexia, but many successful adults call dyslexia their superpower. Dyslexia can lead to unique strengths like creativity, problem-solving abilities, and determination, and she's in good company with famous people like Agatha Christie, Albert Einstein, and Steven Spielberg.[7]

- Yes, it stinks that your daughter's basketball coach isn't giving her much playing time, but she can use this season to get better, cheer on her teammates, and be ready for the day when she's put in a game.

- Yes, it hurts that your daughter didn't get asked to homecoming, but the moms can plan a fun dinner for all the girls who don't have dates. You can go all out—create a balloon arch, set a pretty table, serve their favorite food—and let the girls go to the dance together afterward.

When plan A fails, there are twenty-five other letters in the alphabet. There are many other paths to take.

Whatever circumstances your daughter faces, there is always more than one way to view her situation. There are alternatives to initial assumptions. Learning how to make positive mental pivots now, while she's young and impressionable, is a skill that could become your daughter's greatest superpower. It will serve her *very* well in life.

Avoid the Bitter Barn

On the morning of high school football games, some local football moms meet for a prayer breakfast. They pray for the players' safety and then listen to a speaker.

One morning, an older mom shared her wisdom with the younger moms, saying:

It's easy to get bitter as a football mom. Bitter that your child doesn't get more playing time. Bitter about a holiday practice.

Bitter when the coach changes his position. Bitter about the way the program is run. Here's my advice: Don't get stuck in the bitter barn. Don't get caught up in always complaining, griping, and venting with other moms. Nothing good comes from staying stuck in that place.

The key word here is *stuck*. After all, we're human, and sometimes we vent. Sometimes we make trips to the bitter barn due to legitimate hurts, bad calls, injustices, and human errors.

We all need safe places to process our thoughts and feelings. We need friends who listen and keep our rants in the vault. We also need wise counsel to help us decide when action is needed, because sometimes it is. Sometimes our child needs an advocate.

But staying stuck in the bitter barn, where we keep replaying grievances, is never helpful. Ultimately, it hurts us. Why? Because healthy people eventually leave the bitter barn. They get tired of the negativity and decide it's time to move on.

Guess who is left then? Who likes to get cozy and make a home in the bitter barn? Typically, it's the cynics and doomsayers. People who are always unhappy and would like to convince you that you're unhappy too.

As parents, our perspective rubs off on our children—and so do our coping mechanisms. I saw this firsthand at an eighth-grade basketball game last year. A player on the opposing team, the largest boy on the court, kept pushing boys on our team. When the referee made a call that he didn't like, he lost his mind.

He created such a scene that his coach pulled him out of the game.

Five seconds later, we heard screaming in the stands. This boy's dad was yelling, and his mom stood up to do the same.

Their behavior spiraled, and both parents got so out of control that security had to escort them out. They weren't allowed back into the gym.

Extreme reactions always have a backstory, and when I got home, I wondered about this family's backstory. Did these parents have parents who never taught them emotional regulation? Was this a generational habit? What if their son learned how to control and redirect his anger? Rather than be the team bully, could he be the team leader? Could he use his extra size and strength for *good*?

Life can trigger all of us. We all can act in regrettable ways. We need fortitude to keep our wits about us, and so do our daughters. Fortitude comes from the Holy Spirit. It's a strength we can't manufacture, and when we bite our tongue, act prudently, or refuse to let external conditions determine our behavior, that's fortitude at work.[8] Fortitude gives us the strength of mind to endure a hard situation.

Life will never be perfect on this side of heaven. Certain people and situations may always get under our skin. Knowing this keeps us out of the bitter barn. It helps us prepare our daughters for reality. As Jonathan Pokluda said:

> At any given moment of your life, there are things that are broken and things that are much better than you deserve. You get to choose what you look at and how.
>
> We should work to find the blessings and look at them with gratitude. The broken things will work to distract us from what is right and good. We should look at the broken things with a heart to repair them if possible. If we can't do anything about them, why give them attention?
>
> Here's the hard part, there are things in this world that

will always be broken until Jesus returns. You have to be ok amidst the broken things. Fix what you can and keep going. Keep being thankful. Keep having joy. Don't let the broken moments break you.

Sometimes the broken things will outnumber the blessings, but that is truly only because you're paying more attention to them. In reality, for the Jesus follower, blessings *always* outnumber the broken things. What are you paying attention to?[9]

It's worth considering what your daughter—and you—pay the closest attention to. What occupies your mind? Where do you focus your attention? Research shows that women tend to ruminate more than men and are twice as likely to experience depression.[10] What we dwell on really matters. It affects the road we take at the crossroads of hope and despair.

Your daughter is starting to fight her own mental battles. She may not understand how bitter seeds take root. Be a safe place where she can share her struggles. Admit that you struggle, too, and then hold each other accountable.

To explain how bitterness often begins, share examples like these with your daughter:

- **Envy:** The boy you like asks your best friend on a date. It's okay to feel jealous, but don't dwell there. Don't bad-mouth your friend, forget how much you love her, or wish for a terrible date. Instead, take your heartache to God. Trust that His plan is better than your plan—even if you can't see that yet. Make fun plans with another friend. Remember that boys will come and go, and it's not worth ending a good friendship over a short-term crush.

- **Unmet expectations:** You expect to get invited to a big party, but you don't. You expect your friends to check in on you, but they don't. You love words of affirmation, but your friends don't reciprocate the compliments you give. Many relationship disappointments aren't intentional—they're typically caused by oversight, cluelessness, people being busy, people being self-focused, people juggling problems you can't see, and the fact that not everyone shares your same gifts and skill sets. Everyone has blind spots, and nobody is a mind reader. If your hurt is valid, communicate that with grace to your friend, but always remember that the best way to get out of a rut is to take your eyes off yourself. Go serve, spend time in nature, or show kindness to someone who needs it and will appreciate it.

- **Comparison:** You're okay with getting a hand-me-down car, but seeing the shiny new cars that your best friends get makes you sad. It's okay to feel jealous, but work on feeling grateful. Know that contentment isn't about having what you *want*, but rather, wanting what you *have*. Also, keep a sense of humor by giving your old car a funny nickname that you and your friends can laugh about. You'll have many cars in your lifetime, and not getting your dream car out of the gate gives you something to look forward to. One day, you'll appreciate it more because you had to wait.

- **Pain:** Some older girls at school made insulting remarks about your body. For years you've struggled with body image, and this sets you back. But remember: Not everyone deserves a voice in your life. Not everyone has opinions worth your time and attention. Be careful who you give a megaphone to. Be wise in not letting hurtful people have the loudest voice in your life or live rent-free in your head. As Christine Caine said, "Don't allow what has been done to you to become bigger than what Jesus has done for you!"[11]

Life will always give our daughters a reason to feel bitter, cheated, shaded, or less favored. It will extend an open invitation into the bitter barn. We've all been guilty of visiting this barn on occasion, but let's not stay stuck there. Let's not let life darken our perspective and overshadow our hope and joy. With Jesus, the blessings will always outnumber the broken things. This outlook prepares our daughters to handle setbacks and disappointments.

Remember Gratitude

My daughter Camille came into my office one day searching for supplies.

"Mom, why do you have an EpiPen in your desk?" she asked as she opened a drawer.

"That's the EpiPen we used on you that night at the Greek restaurant," I explained. "I keep it to remember what God did."

Camille nodded, remembering that night well. She spent four hours at Children's of Alabama hospital after having an allergic reaction to zucchini balls that our waitress mistakenly said were safe for her to eat.

Thankfully, Camille felt a tingling reaction in her throat that signaled a problem, and this EpiPen stopped it. I'm forever grateful it worked. I'm forever grateful to the man who invented this device. There's no telling how many lives he has saved.

Yet even with my gratitude, it's hard for me to see this EpiPen. When I think about that night, and the mistake that waitress made, I'm haunted by what could have happened. But I keep this EpiPen to remember God's protection during a frightening event. When I notice it in my drawer, I'm reminded to give thanks.

My guess is that you've had some close calls too. You may have endured a traumatic event that brought you to your knees as you prayed for your child.

Motherhood isn't for sissies, as my mom used to say, and the deeper I get into this journey, the more I realize how we moms have two default modes: *tender* and *tough*. You never know which mode life will call for.

When we hold a baby, we're tender. When we hear hard news, we're tough. Sometimes we're tender and tough at once. Even when we look soft on the outside, we're strong on the inside. We have the heart and spirit of a warrior.

And while we need a positive framework, for ourselves and our daughters, this doesn't mean that God expects us to smile as we face trauma or pretend to like suffering. It doesn't mean that we aren't allowed to sit in sadness, feel our emotions, be angry, or wrestle with the Lord. Even Jesus cried out in the garden of Gethsemane, feeling overwhelmed with sorrow and asking God to remove His suffering if possible, while also accepting God's will (Matthew 26:38–39).

More than anything, God wants us to come to Him. He wants our honesty and authenticity. He can handle seeing our worst because He is God, and nothing we do or say can make us lose His love.

This broken world isn't His original design, and when we cry, He cries. "He comforts us in all our troubles so that we can comfort others" (2 Corinthians 1:4).

Yet even in the mess, even when our minds spin and we can't

think straight, we can praise God's character, faithfulness, promises, and track record. We can gather around the Bible like we would a warm fire, needing it in a deeper, more desperate way.

Dr. David Jeremiah said, "The evidence of God's goodness is everywhere to be seen."[12] Being aware of His hand in any situation is the cornerstone of a healthy outlook.

Being aware of His hand in any situation is the cornerstone of a healthy outlook.

Staying mindful of what He has done in the past—and what He'll continue to do in the future—inspires gratitude.

Gratitude brings perspective. Perspective brings humility. Humility centers us and reminds us that for every blessing we notice, there are a thousand blessings we don't see. We can give thanks for those too.

For most people, gratitude doesn't come naturally. We're more prone to complain. But we can cultivate gratitude by adopting habits like:

- keeping a gratitude journal (or gratitude notes on our phone);
- staying still long enough to notice the red cardinal outside our window that reminds us of a loved one;
- finding extra pleasure in simple joys like a favorite holiday milkshake or watching a father at church kiss his baby;
- training our mind to see the good—like feeling appreciative when we are healthy enough to care for our child after surgery; and
- remembering that someone is praying for the very thing we take for granted. Many people who are deeply hurting would gladly trade problems with us.

Raising daughters in an age of new challenges can tamper with our perspective and test our mental health. It can dishearten us, distract us, and make us miss opportunities to prepare our girls for life beyond our home.

The ripple effect of motherhood is powerful, and the simplest lesson that you teach today could outlive your time on earth. Even a small shift in thinking could feel like an epiphany to your daughter. Most people influence an average of ten thousand people in their lifetime,[13] and helping improve her mental framework could affect the ten thousand lives she'll touch as well. The impact can travel far beyond your home.

Packing perspective in your daughter's suitcase is essential because this is the gift that keeps giving. It will help your daughter and the people she touches become mentally strong and resilient. She can't always control what happens, but she can choose her mindset. She has agency over her point of view and the mentality she brings to the table.

Truths Worth Packing

- "When I was a child, I spoke and thought and reasoned as a child. But when I grew up, I put away childish things." (1 Corinthians 13:11)
- "So we fix our eyes not on what is seen, but on what is unseen, since what is seen is temporary, but what is unseen is eternal." (2 Corinthians 4:18 NIV)

- "There is a way that appears to be right, but in the end it leads to death." (Proverbs 14:12 NIV)
- "Don't copy the behavior and customs of this world, but let God transform you into a new person by changing the way you think. Then you will learn to know God's will for you, which is good and pleasing and perfect." (Romans 12:2)
- "I know how to live on almost nothing or with everything. I have learned the secret of living in every situation, whether it is with a full stomach or empty, with plenty or little. For I can do everything through Christ, who gives me strength." (Philippians 4:12–13)

Questions to Unpack

1. Has your family ever paid the price because someone upset you? How easily do outside influences tamper with your perspective?
2. Has your daughter ever benefitted from a positive framework you shared? What impact did this mental pivot have?
3. Does your family celebrate gratitude? Do you believe gratitude fosters a positive outlook? Why or why not?

—— A Prayer to Lighten Your Load ——

Dear Lord,

Protect my daughter's mental health. Cultivate a healthy perspective. Make her aware of any anxiety, rumination, bitterness, or negative thought loops that make her spiral. Help me get my thinking straight so I can help her. Give us both a healthy outlook that magnifies our blessings and lets us celebrate what is right. I praise You for the eternal perspective that looks beyond today. Help us see the big picture and respond with a thankful heart. In Jesus' name, amen.

CHAPTER 6

DISCERNMENT

STAY AHEAD OF HARD

CONVERSATIONS

*Nothing matters more to me than your
safety. I don't hate fun. I love you.*

DR. LISA DAMOUR

W ow, Mom, that was the best conversation we've ever had!"
I was surprised (and relieved) to hear my daughter's reaction
at the end of a three-hour drive. After all, you never know how well
a tricky conversation will resonate with a seventeen-year-old girl.

We'd just wrapped up an amazing day in Oxford, Mississippi.
We toured the campus of Ole Miss with her best friends and their
moms, and this mother-daughter trip included good food, shopping, and a charming hotel.

The previous night at dinner, we had a fun, grown-up conversation that led the moms to start sharing stories about old

boyfriends. We laughed hysterically, especially as one mom told us about her ex-boyfriend who is now a pilot. Whenever she flies, she's afraid she'll run into him as she exits the plane.

Being on a college campus triggered an avalanche of memories for me. While most of my memories were good, some memories were unsettling, especially through my lens as a mom.

As old experiences came to mind, I realized what my daughter might soon be exposed to. I felt a pressing urge to equip her.

Ever since my daughters were young, I've parented by this motto: "Prepare the child for the road, not the road for the child." I saw it in a magazine when my oldest daughter was a baby. Forewarned is forearmed, and when someone gives us a general lay of the land before we enter that new territory, we're better equipped to make sound choices.

When I was seventeen, I was clueless about the world beyond my home. I was your typical naive girl who went into college blindly. By God's grace, nothing terrible happened, but as I look back, I realize how I could have been a very easy target.

I was raised in an age when parents didn't broach tricky life topics. Most parents back then were shaped by *The Amy Vanderbilt Complete Book of Etiquette*, and if there was an awkward issue, like Uncle Max who got wildly drunk at every family gathering and then suddenly disappeared for two years, it got swept under the rug. The details remained a mystery.

But times have changed, and there is more at stake if we don't prepare our girls for a world where the darkness keeps getting darker and our society has lost its moral code.

Gone are the days where integrity and character are widely valued. Doing the right thing isn't the unspoken norm, and with fewer people living by a moral code—or having a conscience that stops them from harming others—the chance of our daughters being a target is higher than the odds we faced.

Being naive in an age of darkness can have serious consequences, and this is what keeps me brave in initiating hard conversations.

So as my daughter and I drove home from Oxford, I held nothing back. I shed light on the dark realities that she won't hear on a college tour, a job interview, or a date with a sweet-talking guy.

"I love you," I said, "and I will *not* let you leave home clueless like I did. Buckle up because I'm about to share the nitty-gritty details of life after high school. I want you to know what you're up against."

For three hours, we talked nonstop, going back and forth. Before we knew it, we were back at home. It felt like the fastest car ride ever.

Early in the conversation, my daughter was quiet. She listened as I touched on a mixed bag of topics that included:

- binge drinking, drugs, and stomachs getting pumped at the hospital;
- sexual promiscuity, STDs, and the hook-up culture;
- sexual assault, sex trafficking, and date rape drugs slipped into drinks;
- depression, suicide, and mental health;
- pornography;
- drinking and driving;
- eating disorders—anorexia, orthorexia, and bulimia;
- mean girls, predatory guys, and when to leave a party or a date;
- loneliness, anxiety, and self-doubt;
- discernment and trusting your gut instincts;

- making good choices while not judging others;
- the importance of family, faith, and true friends; and
- God's unconditional love and mercy.

I shared stories of what I'd seen or heard. She shared stories, too, including a sad story about a friend from another school who she'd met through a Bible study. The year before, this girl had gotten a bad reputation for being promiscuous. She confessed to this group that she'd been sexually assaulted, and that trauma led to some terrible decisions.

I told my daughter how I once read that victims of abuse often struggle to set boundaries. They feel like they are "public property," that their resources, body, and time should be available to others just for the asking.[1] Given this, it's easy to see why some girls become promiscuous when they suddenly view their body as if it belongs to everyone else.

This led to another great conversation about not jumping to conclusions or judging anyone when they make poor choices, because you never know their backstory. By showing compassion, you may help them heal, change their course, and discover God's grace.

Hockey legend Wayne Gretzky once said, "I skate to where the puck is going to be, not where it has been."[2] As parents, we do the same thing. We anticipate what's around the corner for our children. We watch to see where the puck is headed—and then we give them a heads-up.

This strategy shapes today's conversations. It makes tricky talks less awkward. It's easier to talk about dating before your daughter has a boyfriend. It's easier to talk about drinking before she's pressured at a party.

With this next generation growing up fast, hard conversations may be needed sooner than we think. Don't worry if you feel like you're late, because it's never too late to start these conversations that will continue for many years.

My daughter was in ninth grade when a friend hosted a party with alcohol. The parents were out of town, but what I often hear now (from moms in different communities) is that some parents *serve* alcohol at parties for ninth graders. After a homecoming dance at one school, all the ninth-grade girls were vomiting at an after-party in someone's home.

If the thought of these talks feels overwhelming, remember this: Nobody is a pro at first. Nobody nails it on day one, especially if your parents never modeled it for you.

My first conversation was extremely awkward, and my daughter agrees. She jokingly recalls it as one of her most traumatic childhood experiences.

Apparently, she dreaded this talk all week after seeing it scheduled on my calendar: *Sex talk, 6:00 p.m. Monday.* We laughed hysterically as she shared this recently, and I told her there is great truth to the saying that the oldest child gets the best of the grandparenting and the worst of the parenting. In every new stage of growing up, the firstborn is the guinea pig.

My husband and I were amateurs with our first conversations. We had no game or clever strategy. But we kept being proactive. We gained confidence as we tried different scripts.

Nobody can predict every dilemma that our daughters will face. We won't always have the perfect words. But we can control the narrative as the most trusted adult in their lives. We can address the realities we know they'll encounter at some point in time.

Let your daughter hear it from *you*. Establish yourself as the authority. Even if you're nervous . . . even if your voice shakes . . . even if you feel sick to your stomach . . . an imperfect conversation is always better than no conversation at all.

With practice, you'll get better. You'll also get a pulse on how to read your child.

My three-hour car talk with my daughter never would have happened if she didn't engage with me. What set the stage for that long conversation were many awkward conversations that came before it. The timing felt appropriate, too, as it made sense to talk about college after a campus tour.

As moms, we want to protect our daughters' innocence. We want to shelter them from harsh realities as long as we can, and this desire is good.

And while we shouldn't rush the hard conversations, or share too many dark details too soon, we also can't neglect the truth. Parents who keep an open dialogue often have children who feel comfortable opening up to them. Parents who avoid these difficult topics often have kids who seek guidance from the internet or from their friends.

We can be *realistic* yet *optimistic* as we prepare our girls for the road ahead. Use the stolen moments you have, like a ten-minute car ride to school or a visit to the doctor, to prepare your daughter for tricky terrain and foster the discernment she needs.

Will You Let God Equip You?

Imagine momentarily all the challenges you faced at your daughter's age. Remember the insecurities you felt related to your appearance, your body, your performance, your achievements, your social life, your dating life, and so on.

Now imagine these challenges multiplied. Add in social media, cyberbullying, cancel culture, the pressure to be perfect, the pressure to be an influencer, seeing every party you're *not* invited to, polarizing politics, violence, a hypersexualized society, gender confusion, and a host of other modern-day issues shaping the next generation.

The worst part is, our girls don't feel safe. Many girls say their biggest fear is getting kidnapped and forced into sex trafficking. Even at church, our girls see police protection outside. They visit a friend in college and get advised by the older girls to always watch their drink because people will slip in drugs. They carry pepper spray and Tasers to keep themselves safe.

In short, our daughters are being shaped by a darker world than the world that shaped us. God is good, but evil is real, and until the day that Jesus returns, we live in a spiritual war zone. As Priscilla Shirer said in her *Armor of God* Bible study, Satan may be invisible, but he's not fictional.[3] There are dark powers we can't always see.

> *God is good, but evil is real, and until the day that Jesus returns, we live in a spiritual war zone.*

Thankfully, there is hope. While we should be aware of the darkness, we don't have to be consumed. Shirer also said:

> Being a believer doesn't give you immunity from the assaults of the enemy, but it does give you access to the power of the Father—His power to defend you as well as reverse what's been done to you. If you want to win the fight—if you want to join me in flipping the script, pinning down the enemy, and crippling his impact in your life—the key is realizing you're connected to more spiritual brawn than is coming against you.[4]

Raising girls today requires a dichotomy of messages. When my daughters were young, I emphasized the good things. *Be kind. Be compassionate. Be a good friend. Show the fruit of the Holy Spirit.*

But as they grew up, the conversations evolved. I found myself also saying: *Keep your head on a swivel. Trust your gut. Have eyes in the back of your head. You can be rude to keep yourself safe. If someone's hurting you, do whatever it takes to escape. Don't let anyone take advantage of you or walk all over you. Know how to stand up for yourself.*

All the while, I've wondered: How do we raise our daughters in the light—yet prepare them for the dark? How do we help them handle hard realities without letting reality harden them?

Thankfully, we aren't alone. God equips us as each new season of motherhood builds on the season before.

As a young mom, you aren't ready to parent a teenager or a young adult. But with time and experience, your readiness grows.

If you look too far ahead or rely too much on yourself, you'll feel overwhelmed. The challenges will seem insurmountable. But if you focus on today, you'll find God. He is found in the present, and by listening to what He says today, hard conversations feel doable. You'll get the wisdom you need for now.

And let this bring you additional relief: Hard conversations shouldn't happen all at once. They aren't a "one and done" deal anymore.

Rather than share everything your daughter should know in one weekend, which can feel like drinking water from a fire hose, share sound bites. Use a story that fits into your normal conversation. Talk about an issue in small, short, age-appropriate doses.

The drip, drip, drip method, used by my friends at Birds &

Bees, works better than one big talk.[5] Just as your daughter could never learn AP chemistry all at once, she can't learn about real life in one sitting either. It's better—and more effective—to offer small doses that build up and feel easier to digest.

The goal of small conversations is to slowly inoculate our girls. To gradually grow their tolerance to handle the rough elements of this fallen world. Only with God's help is this possible, so let's tune into His counsel. Let's pay attention to what He says.

Appeal to Your Daughter's Logic

My friend's daughter was a high school senior, and like most seniors, she had one foot out the door.

She asked to take a beach trip with her friends over a long holiday weekend. Normally, her mom would say yes, but this request was different. Boys were invited, too, and they'd all stay under the same roof with a single dad and his girlfriend as their chaperones.

It was a bad idea, but my friend didn't overreact. Instead, she empathized. She knew her daughter would be upset as the only one who couldn't go.

"Why?" her daughter argued. "You know I can do this next year when I'm in college."

"Yes," her mom replied, "and when that time comes *next year*, I want you to remember my answer *this year*."

To me, that's good parenting. That's teaching a girl how to think for herself and not blindly follow the crowd.

My friend didn't bad-mouth the other parents' decisions or sacrifice her convictions. She didn't fuel her daughter's frustration by giving her a lecture. Instead, she planned a fun family trip that same weekend. She put a voice in her daughter's head that she'll need as she leaves home.

These moments of tension are hard to endure, but relationships can survive them when they're deeply rooted in love. This same friend tells her children, "Your dad and I are your team captains. If anything happens, good or bad, we're your first phone call. Come to us *first*."

Even when her kids don't like her decisions, they know they can trust her love. They're confident that their parents are solidly on their team.

This confidence is key. Before hard conversations ever begin, our girls need to know that we have their backs. We truly want what is best for them long term. Even if they mess up and we get upset, we'll get over it. But what we'd never get over is something terrible happening to them or someone else.

How we approach a hard conversation makes a difference in whether we're heard. In this book's appendix, I've listed twenty-five talks worth having, scripts to get you started in preparing your daughter for the road ahead. Take what you want, and let my ideas inspire your ideas. Every family has its own values, and your values will shape your narrative.

When you feel tempted to avoid a tricky topic, remember the goal is to set the first tracks. The concept of "setting the first tracks" is best explained by this analogy:

Imagine your daughter at the top of a ski slope. She looks down the mountain and sees a fresh blanket of snow. It's beautiful, perfect, and flawless. There isn't a blemish in sight. That snow is like her young mind. It's innocent and pristine. But soon, skiers will come down and set tracks in the snow. Whoever sets the *first* tracks will leave a particularly deep impression. Your daughter won't forget her first exposure. She'll always remember those first tracks.

As a parent, you want to set the first tracks. You want to ski down *first* and impress God's truth in your daughter's mind so that when other skiers come down behind you, your daughter knows which tracks to trust. She remembers what you once said.

The window of an innocent childhood keeps getting smaller. At incredibly young ages, girls now get exposed to controversial messages that undermine traditional family values. Be intentional in showing your daughter which tracks she can trust. Be her go-to person as you set a loving baseline of truth.

Ask God to Fill in Your Parenting Gap

Nobody has a crystal ball regarding the future. We can't predict or prepare our girls for every scenario they'll face. Our power as moms is limited. We can do only so much.

Thankfully, God is sovereign. He is present when we are not. When you feel overwhelmed, pray this: *Jesus, be the gap between what my child needs and what I can give. Meet her at the end of my limitations.*

God often uses other people to fill in our parenting gap. He uses outside influences—special teachers, coaches, mentors, aunts, uncles, moms, grandparents, and others—to give our daughters what they need through their wisdom and unique strengths.

It takes humility to embrace these influences. No parent is equipped to be their child's be-all and end-all, so ask God to work through others when you fall short.

Whatever I forgot, failed, or neglected to teach my daughters, I pray that their friends' parents did teach them. And when my daughters encounter a new situation that they don't know how to handle, I pray they'll have a friend nearby who is ready because of their parents' teaching or coaching.

This is how we help one another. This is how God's kingdom grows. What we pour into our daughters today, they'll pour into one another tomorrow. What a beautiful dynamic to imagine. What a wonderful way to help our daughters become a blessing to one another.

As moms, we need our age-and-stage friends. We also need mom friends who have older girls and are several steps ahead of us. These "been there, done that" friends are invaluable. One, they're quick to share their mistakes. Two, they possess the gift of hindsight. Three, they help us stay calm when we want to panic. And four, they prepare us for the road ahead. They make us better guides for our children.

Our daughters need grace *and* grit in their journey to adulthood. We should cultivate a love for what is good. We should praise what is excellent, true, honorable, right, pure, lovely, and admirable (Philippians 4:8). At the same time, we can prepare our girls for life beyond our home by helping them feel ready for, not blindsided by, the things that aren't from God.

> *Our daughters need grace and grit in their journey to adulthood.*

As Charles Spurgeon is credited with saying, "Discernment is not knowing the difference between right and wrong; it is knowing the difference between right and almost right." Even the shiniest opportunity or most seemingly perfect relationship will never end well if it's not from God. Let's give our daughters a leg up in life by offering a lay of the land and describing what they may see as they journey into new territory.

Packing discernment in your daughter's suitcase is essential because it prepares her for the road ahead. It magnifies God's quiet voice and helps her tune into her feelings of hesitation and moments that give her pause. By not shying away from hard conversations and by letting your daughter hear the truth from you, you build trust in your relationship. You bring clarity into an age of confusion and light into the darkness.

Truths Worth Packing

- "Now go! I will be with you as you speak, and I will instruct you in what to say." (Exodus 4:12)
- "If you need wisdom, ask our generous God, and he will give it to you. He will not rebuke you for asking." (James 1:5)
- "Dear friends, do not believe everyone who claims to speak by the Spirit. You must test them to see if the spirit they have comes from God. For there are many false prophets in the world." (1 John 4:1)
- "Put on the full armor of God, so that you can take your stand against the devil's schemes. For our struggle is not against flesh and blood, but against the rulers, against the authorities, against the powers of this dark world and against the spiritual forces of evil in the heavenly

realms. Therefore put on the full armor of God, so that when the day of evil comes, you may be able to stand your ground, and after you have done everything, to stand." (Ephesians 6:11–13 NIV)

- "But the LORD said to Samuel, 'Do not consider his appearance or his height, for I have rejected him. The LORD does not look at the things people look at. People look at the outward appearance, but the LORD looks at the heart.'" (1 Samuel 16:7 NIV)

Questions to Unpack

1. What are your top three priorities in preparing your daughter for life? Do you agree with the adage "Prepare your child for the road, not the road for your child"?

2. How comfortable do you feel initiating hard conversations? What postponed conversation should you address soon?

3. Describe a time when you "set the first tracks" to establish a baseline of truth. What happened as your daughter heard conflicting information? Did your early conversation prevent some confusion as she sorted through different narratives? Why or why not?

A Prayer to Lighten Your Load

Dear Lord,
Build my daughter's discernment. Strengthen her aware-
ness, intuition, and instincts. Open her heart to guidance
and direction from the right people. Give me the words for
hard conversations and tell me when to have them. Present
opportunities for me to impress the truth on my daughter's
heart. I praise You for the privilege of getting her ready for
life. Please prepare me as I prepare her. In Jesus' name I
pray, amen.

CHAPTER 7

CONNECTION

GROW YOUR INFLUENCE

AS YOU LOSE CONTROL

We want a leader who can say, "You're allowed to
be upset; your emotional storm isn't overwhelming
my sense of what's right here. I am still your
sturdy leader." . . . We are the pilots of our family.
Our kids look to us for love and leadership.

DR. BECKY KENNEDY

To this day, I'm not sure how my father remained unfazed.

I was in my early twenties and reeling from a breakup. I'd just come home for my sister's engagement party, and honestly, I had the best time. I danced, laughed, and played the good-sister role among all our family friends.

But when I crawled into bed that night, the sadness returned with a vengeance. I knew this breakup was right, yet I'd been crying for weeks, and in the safety of my childhood home, the tears turned into a waterfall.

I missed the thrill of when we first started dating. I couldn't imagine being happy without him. But staying together made me miserable too. I felt lonely, stuck, and confused.

In the darkness of my bedroom, my emotions crashed down, and my sadness hit a peak. For lack of a better idea, I tiptoed into my parents' bedroom. They were both asleep, so I woke up my dad. In between my sobbing tears, I asked if he'd lie down with me. Without a moment of hesitation, he said yes.

My dad stayed steady as I cried and fell asleep in his arms. He didn't ask me a dozen questions. He didn't hound me to explain what was wrong. He didn't panic or freak out because this breakdown was out of character for me. Never in my life had I fallen apart this way.

Instead, my dad held me, loved me, and made me feel like this heartache would end. He gave me the security I needed—with no explanation needed.

Looking back, I see that night as a turning point. It instilled the strength and confidence I needed to keep moving forward. Knowing my dad, he probably prayed as he held me. Any strength I felt the next morning was probably the Holy Spirit helping me fight the urge to return to that relationship. I'm so thankful I didn't cave due to a sadness that would pass.

Today, I remember this story as I raise my own daughters. It reminds me of the parent I hope to be.

I can't solve all their problems, erase all their pain, or predict what will make them cry on their pillow, but I can be a steady presence. I can help them survive their darkest days and nights without panicking or demanding immediate explanations.

But for my girls to seek my help, or want my help in the first place, a strong relationship is needed. We've got to have that connection before a heartache ever hits. After all, my daughters and yours have more choices of who to turn to and listen to than any previous generation. They get exposed to more voices in *one day* than we heard in *one year* at their age, thanks to social media.

Our daughters don't care what we know until they know that we care.

Our daughters don't care what we know until they know that we care, and especially as they prepare to leave home, we often find ourselves on the outside looking in, trying to be part of their new world that doesn't always include us.

At this point, we must earn a voice in their lives. We start competing with additional voices and influences, including some that are anti-family.

It saddens me to hear about a new cultural trend of young people who cut their parents out of their life. A recent article noted that "the rise in millennials and Gen Zers coming forward to discuss their own crises—the hashtag #ToxicFamily has 1.9 billion views on TikTok—may suggest that American families are severing ties at an all-time high."[1]

To be fair, some families *are* toxic. Some parents are harmful, and boundaries are needed as the children leave home. But as the word *toxic* gets overused (and incorrectly applied) in our current culture, many young people find themselves in a very lonely place. They listen to influencers who tell them to write off people at the drop of a hat, and before long they've written off everyone. They have no loyal or long-term relationships.

Nobody who has their back.

Nobody who loves them deeply.

Nobody they can wake up at midnight when their sadness hits a peak.

Our daughters desire a good relationship with us. They long for the security of a loving and stable home. The key to connection as they mature is to grow our influence as we lose control—and keep their hearts soft and open to us.

In his book *The Key to Your Child's Heart*, Gary Smalley used sea anemones to illustrate this point. As a young boy, he loved to watch these creatures. Sea anemones have soft and wavy tentacles, and when he poked them with a stick, he noticed how they withdrew their sensitive tentacles. They closed up into a shell to protect themselves from further injury.

A person's spirit reacts the same way, Smalley noted. It's open and vulnerable to begin with, but when it gets poked, it closes up. The most prevalent cause of disharmony in a home is a closed spirit, Smalley said. "The greater the harshness, the greater the pain a person feels in his spirit."[2]

We've all been poked by someone we love. We've been so hurt by their words and actions (or their *lack* of action) that we've withdrawn and put up walls because we didn't feel safe and secure.

I've seen my daughters retreat into their shell because I lost my temper, asked too many questions, said something hurtful, got overly emotional, put too much pressure on them, or failed to listen and consider how they felt. I've noticed how they invite me in when I listen calmly, think before I speak, ask how I can help them, and truly enjoy their company. The older they get, the more time I spend in mentor mode, friend mode, and counselor mode.

Rather than fear the control I've lost, I've grown to love the connection we've gained. It's a deeper, richer, more meaningful relationship.

Our daughters want us to stay engaged in their lives—but they don't want us running the show. They long to express their emotions and dilemmas without seeing us sound the alarm. They rely on our strength when they lack their own. They crave our love even when they become a hot mess.

Parenting with influence keeps us connected. It sets the stage for a lifelong friendship and builds a bridge that brings our daughters home. Even in the early years, it's worth noticing what keeps your daughter's heart open. It's worth every minute you spend growing a relationship where she trusts you as her sturdy leader.

How Do You Respond to Disappointing Choices?

I often hear from moms whose hearts are broken over the choices their young adult daughter has made.

Their pain is understandable, especially when the relationship has taken a hit. Some moms feel so upset they struggle to show love to their daughter. They're stuck in a place of wondering:

Where did I go wrong?
Why is she rejecting the values we taught her?
What hardened her heart toward God?
What happened to her? She wasn't like this when she
    left home.

I'll tell you what happened: She entered a culture that glamorizes sin and has deeply confused this next generation. It's a world where things like sexual promiscuity, living with your boyfriend, pornography, drugs, rejecting your faith upbringing, and family estrangement get normalized and celebrated.

It sounds counterintuitive, but our girls need our love the most when they're hardest to love. They need our influence even more when their idea of normal gets twisted.

While some situations call for drastic measures, like when their safety is at stake, the most common dilemma is knowing how to address the elephant in the room. How do you talk about choices that break your heart? How do you express legitimate concerns? How do you remind your daughter that she was made for more than the lifestyle this world promotes?

Here are seven reminders to take to heart before you take action:

1. **Remember to have fun.** Taking all the joy out of your relationship will make your daughter tune out. As my fourteen-year-old once told me, "Mom, if you make every conversation a life lesson, I'm going to stop listening." To this day, I keep her words in mind.

   Spend more time connecting with your daughter than correcting her, especially if you're struggling to love her. Plan a fun weekend getaway or spend the night at a cool hotel. Get massages together, take a cooking class, make s'mores by the bonfire, and watch your favorite movie. Laugh and make memories as you find common ground over something as simple as rocky road ice cream. Enjoy your daughter's company with no strings attached. Remember how much you loved her as a baby and a toddler.

Having lighthearted fun together strengthens your relationship. It gets your heart in the right place, builds trust, and opens the door for your daughter to *want* to listen to you. This approach works better (and feels better) than harping on what upsets you and fixating to the point that it pushes her away. It improves your odds of being heard.

2. **Remember that every human is one mistake away from falling off a cliff.** We're all sinners who fall short of God's glory (Romans 3:23). Your daughter's mistakes may look different from yours, but sin is sin, and remembering your own sin keeps your heart tender. It prevents pride or anger from taking over. Check yourself so you don't act morally superior. Coming across as holier-than-thou will stop a conversation fast, especially with a teenage daughter.

3. **Remember that when God looks at your daughter, He sees her beautiful potential. He sees who she can be.** Even if her current choices crush you, you can see your daughter's potential. You can speak into that vision.

   Many parents grow distraught when their "perfect Christian daughter" leaves home and strays. One mom asked me, "How can I love her when it hurts to look at her?" When she sees her daughter, her mistakes jump out.

   It's an honest feeling, but if I ever felt that way, I'd tell myself this: *Now isn't the time to talk to my daughter. Now isn't the time to raise concerns. Instead, it's time for me to talk to God—and get my heart straight. Until I feel genuine love for my daughter, until I can see her like her Creator sees her, anything I say will be hurtful and do more damage than good.*

4. **Remember that your daughter's choices aren't about you—or what people think.** It's easy to take her poor choices

personally. It's easy to fixate on questions like *How could she do this to me?* and grow emotionally absent. But your daughter needs you, and her health and relationship with God are far more important than what anyone thinks about her or you. Don't let your confidence depend on whether you look like a rock-star mom. Instead, focus on your daughter's well-being. Get her any help she needs and remember that love wants what is best for a person long term. Love keeps the big picture in mind.

5. **Remember that only God can change a heart.** Your daughter has free will, and even if you could parent perfectly, you can't be her Holy Spirit. You can't shame her into salvation or let her piggyback on yours. God has children, not grandchildren, and there comes a point where your daughter must own her faith and make it her personal choice.

   Pray for God to reveal Himself. Pray for godly voices to come around her. And when you feel the urge to "fix" your daughter, get on your knees instead. The battle for her heart is won in prayer.

6. **Remember that wise words help keep her heart open. Aim to speak the truth in love.** Proverbs 16:24 says, "Kind words are like honey—sweet to the soul and healthy for the body." Being too blunt will make your daughter defensive, so speak intentionally. Rather than tell her, "Your new style is ridiculous. Why are you dressing like a streetwalker?" you could say, "I love you, and I'm very concerned about recent changes I've noticed. Is there something I should know about? My instinct tells me there is."

   Maybe her friends all dress this way to get dates or attention. Maybe she feels insecure and desperate for a boyfriend. Maybe she wants to show off her body because she finally likes the way it looks. Help her tap into her self-awareness. Have her think about the way her choices make her feel. Learning this skill will keep her accountable to herself.

7. **Remember that your daughter won't always take your advice, even when you're right.** So when she faces the fallout of a bad decision, sit with her in the misery. Avoid the urge to say, "I told you so." Doing so facilitates trust. It makes her more likely to come to you again.

In his book *Doing Life with Your Adult Children*, Jim Burns shared a story about Ruth "Bunny" Graham, daughter of the late Billy Graham, being shown grace by her parents in her rock-bottom moment. Bunny had been married for eighteen years when she learned that her husband, who worked for her father and with whom she had three kids, was living a secret life of infidelity. She felt devastated and suicidal. A few months later, she married a guy on the rebound against her parents' counsel. Within a day she realized her mistake, and with her life in shambles, she packed up her belongings, fled her abusive marriage, and started driving.

Not knowing where to go, Bunny swallowed her pride and went to her parents' home. They'd warned her not to marry this man, yet home still felt like the safest refuge. As Bunny approached home, she felt nervous and ashamed. She wondered how her parents would respond. For security purposes, their home had gates, so she called to tell her parents that she was coming.

As the gates opened, she immediately saw her father, Billy Graham, waiting for her. He embraced her with a bear hug and said, "Welcome home, Bunny." Rather than lecture his daughter or condemn her for making a mistake, he offered love and grace. Both her parents helped her heal "not by what they said but by what they didn't say."[3]

Whatever issues cause your heart to break, Burns said the question in the heart of every adult child is, "Do you still love me?" He noted that "although it can take a great deal of discipline, we can shower our adult kids with love even when they wander off the path we had hoped for them. God's love for us is the perfect example of the unconditional love we must strive to lavish on our children."[4]

The connection we build with our daughters—and whether they come back home once they leave home—is largely determined by how well we handle their disappointing choices. We can hold them to high standards and still leave zero doubt that we'll be there if they fall.

To be loved when you feel unlovable is a major game changer. Our daughters won't forget these moments, these core memories that play on repeat, when a parent passes away. In the end, unconditional love stands out. This is what our daughters will remember most.

Perhaps that's why this Instagram post resonated with me:

RELIGION: "I MESSED UP. MY DAD IS GONNA KILL ME."
GOSPEL: "I MESSED UP. I NEED TO CALL MY DAD."[5]

When our daughters bring their problems to us, it shows that we have influence. We have a chance to speak into their lives while their hearts are still open.

We can't make them always listen. We can't save them from every peril. But we can love them when they're hard to love. We can sit with them when things don't go well and help them rebuild their life. Most of all, we can follow the lead of a God who is rich in mercy and extends an open invitation for us to come home.

Build a Healthy Connection

One challenge we face in raising daughters today is finding a healthy balance in our mother-daughter connection.

While we don't want to engage too little, we don't want to engage too much either. As the old saying goes: *Never do for your child what they can do for themselves—or almost do for themselves.* This is how we raise independent girls who can handle life without us.

The current trend is to over parent. To not cut the cord in places where we can and should. Getting too invested in your daughter's life can stunt her growth. It can foster a relationship where she can't function without calling you twenty times a day—or where you might feel justified in calling her boss for making her work on her birthday.

Clearly, we don't want to swing that far. We don't want to create codependence. But what often happens when you know the daily details of your daughter's life is the lines slowly blur. You stop seeing where her life ends and your life begins.

This explains why I've found myself saying, "*We* have a test on Friday . . . *We* are trying out for the dance team . . . *We* just made the dance team! . . . *We* are really struggling . . . *We* are studying for the ACT." Being plugged into my daughters' lives can make their emotions and my emotions run together.

My favorite story comes from a counselor who saw a mother and daughter at Starbucks both sobbing and falling apart. The mom told this counselor, "*We* are so upset because *we* just broke up with our boyfriend!"

It's a funny example yet relatable too. While I love that moms today are more engaged than previous generations, this can create a codependency where our well-being depends on theirs. And when your daughter faces a heartache, you may become a bigger wreck than her—and lose influence as you fail to provide the emotional support she needs.

I've certainly been guilty of this, and when I need a reset, I remind myself that no child wants to be the strongest person in the room. As parents, we're called to be bigger, stronger, wiser, and kind.

The bigger, stronger, wiser, and kind concept comes from the Circle of Security,[6] which my counselor friend Kim Anderson uses. It's an attachment theory that allows kids to draw strength and enjoy life through their relationship with us. A healthy attachment helps our daughters feel more freedom and confidence to explore the world while knowing that we delight in watching them and welcome them back anytime.

Practically speaking, imagine it this way: Your daughter is upset, and her emotions are flying. They are up, down, and wildly unpredictable. You've seen this before, and you know what's coming. She's jumping on the emotional roller coaster. You're tempted to jump on too.

The old you would join that crazy ride where your emotions spin out of control with hers. But this time, you choose differently.

You remember how your last ride made you feel anxious and exhausted, and you're determined to be a sturdy leader. You want a healthy connection with your daughter.

So rather than mirror your daughter's reaction, you stay on the platform. You hug her, let her vent, and resist the urge to "fix" whatever makes her sad. You respond in a way that tells her, "I'm not getting on that roller coaster with you, but I will be here on the platform, waiting for you with my arms wide open when you're ready to get off."

That is the mom that girls today need. And that is a healthy way to connect.

Will we always get it right? Will we always choose the ideal response? Of course not. Sometimes we jump on the emotional roller coaster because we just can't help ourselves!

But it helps to know the goal. It helps to have a friend who keeps a sense of humor and joins us as we laugh at ourselves. Two moms I know have a running joke when one of their daughters starts to test them. They tell each other, "Stay on the platform, Mom! Stay on the platform!" We need that lightheartedness and moral support. We need friends who get our struggles.

Some days when you try to connect, your daughter won't connect back. Instead of getting the hug you need, you may get a mood swing, a snarky comment, or a bad attitude. To stay bigger, stronger, wiser, and kind, you've got to receive love too. You can't always rely on a child for that. You can't expect your daughter to always reciprocate.

This is where your faith comes in. This is where you let God love *you* so you can love your daughter. I also recommend building your adult village. Leaning into the love of someone you trust (your spouse, your best friend, your mom, your sister, your neighbor, your tennis partner, whomever) keeps you strong for your daughter so her emotions don't shake you. It fosters a healthy attachment where you can sit with her as she wrestles with pain.

Clinical psychologist and author Dr. Lisa Damour said, "Remaining calm when teenagers become undone communicates the critical point that we are not frightened by their acute discomfort, and so they don't need to be frightened by it either."[7]

Let's be honest: It's hard not to mirror your daughter's emotions. It's easy to blur the lines between her life and yours. But the older she gets, the more inner strength and steadiness she needs from you. Make it your goal to be bigger, stronger, wiser, and kind. Build a healthy connection by giving her a secure home base and waiting with open arms for her to come back to you.

Be Your Daughter's Biggest Cheerleader

It was our last spring break as a family of six, and I wanted to make it special. I planned a fun trip to the Florida Keys.

My oldest daughter, a high school senior, had grown tight with her best friends. They planned a last-minute beach trip, and she begged me to let her go. Since our plans were set, that wasn't an option. I felt confident she'd enjoy our vacation so much that she'd forget about her friends' invitation.

We had an amazing week, but halfway through it, I looked over one afternoon and noticed sadness on my daughter's face as she scrolled through Instagram and saw her best friends together at the beach.

I knew what she was thinking. She wished that she could be with them. And at first, it hurt my feelings. I took it personally.

Were we not good enough? Fun enough? Exciting enough? Couldn't she appreciate the effort, money, and love I invested in this trip?

But after taking a minute to reflect, I realized something new: My daughter was ready to leave home and expand her horizons. I couldn't stop this train if I wanted to. She had proclaimed her readiness on many occasions, excitedly telling me, "I can't wait to go to college!" And truly, I'd felt excited for her. But this moment felt different. This felt *real*. She was ready to spread her wings, and the bigger question was, Was I ready to let her go?

This moment was my catalyst to embrace my new role as my daughter's biggest cheerleader. It's when I began a new chapter of growing my influence as I lost control.

Since then, I've learned this: In your daughter's final year at home, you only feel the loss. You feel sad about all the changes and every "last" of senior year. You can't imagine new joy on the other side because that joy doesn't exist yet. It hasn't been revealed.

But new joy is coming—and so are new blessings. There will be great opportunities to deepen your connection with your daughter as you cheer for her, advise her, and keep her moving forward. She needs your positivity, encouragement, and assurance that she is ready for each new beginning because she will doubt herself. She will need reminders that she can do what scares her, whether that's choosing a hard major, running for student government, scheduling a doctor's appointment, or giving a speech in front of fifty people.

You won't agree with every choice she makes, but you can be a safe place for your daughter. You can aim to lighten her load. Girls tend to be very hard on themselves, and as your daughter adds extra pressure to her suitcase by not feeling smart enough, pretty enough, perfect enough, or successful enough, she needs you to set the record straight.

She needs you to call out what she is doing *right* and what false narratives she needs to unload.

She needs you to call out what she is doing right and what false narratives she needs to unload.

As you ease her burdens, you strengthen your connection. You gain more influence in her life. Jim Burns said, "If you build a relationship of positivity and respect, cheer on your adult children, and then wait, they will seek out your advice."[8] I agree, and I also agree with his observation that one great benefit of adult children is developing a deeper friendship. The key is knowing when to bite our tongues and not expressing every thought we have. Rather than vocalize everything we disagree with, we can cheer for the things we affirm.[9]

The day your daughter leaves home isn't the last time she'll seek your help or your advice. In some ways, she'll need you more. She'll have bigger choices to make and larger consequences at stake. Especially in her early twenties—when she's told the world is her oyster, yet the choices feel overwhelming—she needs extra guidance. She needs a sturdy leader to help her find her way.

Packing connection in your daughter's suitcase is essential because it builds the bridge that draws her home. It inspires a lifelong friendship. Most importantly, it gives your daughter a sense of security for her worst moments and darkest nights. It reminds her that there is no problem bigger than your love for her.

Truths Worth Packing

- "A wise woman builds her home, but a foolish woman tears it down with her own hands." (Proverbs 14:1)
- "For where two or three gather in my name, there am I with them." (Matthew 18:20 NIV)
- "She is clothed with strength and dignity, and she laughs without fear of the future. When she speaks, her words are wise, and she gives instructions with kindness. She carefully watches everything in her household and suffers nothing from laziness. Her children stand and bless her. Her husband praises her: 'There are many virtuous and capable women in the world, but you surpass them all!'" (Proverbs 31:25–29)
- "Suppose one of you has a hundred sheep and loses one of them. Doesn't he leave the ninety-nine in the open country and go after the lost sheep until he finds it? . . . I tell you that in the same way there will be more rejoicing in heaven over one sinner who repents than over ninety-nine righteous persons who do not need to repent." (Luke 15:4, 7 NIV)
- "Let us think of ways to motivate one another to acts of love and good works. And let us not neglect our meeting together, as some people do, but encourage one another, especially now that the day of his return is drawing near." (Hebrews 10:24–25)

Questions to Unpack

1. Name a person who once helped you survive a stormy time or a dark night. What did they teach you about being a sturdy leader?
2. How often do you join your daughter's emotional roller coaster? What does "staying on the platform" look like to you?
3. Where can you relinquish control in your daughter's life? Where can you gain influence? What hobbies could you enjoy together as a connection point?

A Prayer to Lighten Your Load

Dear Lord,
Deepen the connection between my daughter and me. Help me become a wise guide and a trusted voice. In her lowest moments, draw closer to her. Let her feel Your compassion, mercy, and abundant love. I praise You for setting the perfect example of how to love my daughter well. Help me grow my influence in every new season of life. In Jesus' name, amen.

CHAPTER 8

PURPOSE

ENCOURAGE A MISSION MINDSET

*Desire that your life count for something
great! Long for your life to have eternal
significance. Want this! Don't coast
through life without a passion.*

JOHN PIPER

Jon Sundt's mission began with two tragedies that hit far too close to home.

He experienced a family's worst nightmare as he lost two brothers to drug addiction. Determined to turn his personal trauma into positive change, he created a nonprofit organization called Natural High to help young people make better decisions.[1]

Through Natural High, middle school and high school students are encouraged to choose a "natural high" over drugs and alcohol. They hear messages rooted in storytelling from role models and key influencers.

I learned about Jon and the Natural High program through Bethany Hamilton's Mother/Daughter Program, now part of the Bethany Hamilton Network.[2] Shortly after I spoke to this group about building strong friendships, Jon spoke on drug prevention and substance abuse.

Immediately he captured our hearts and attention as he shared childhood photos of him with his brothers. They looked like happy, carefree siblings, and seeing this normalcy at the start of his family's journey made his message feel real and relevant. The devastation that comes with addiction can happen to *any* family.

Jon explained how we are all designed to experience "natural highs" in life. We all have passions that bring us alive and help us give life to others—gifts like music, sports, science, filmmaking, and other healthy interests.

Sometimes, however, especially in dark or difficult seasons, we choose artificial highs instead of natural highs. We turn to drugs, alcohol, food, shopping, technology, or another quick fix to give us the joy, peace, or euphoria we crave.

As a Natural High spokesperson, Bethany Hamilton told the girls in her program that her natural high is surfing. It's what she was born to do. After she lost an arm in a shark attack as a young girl, it would have been easy to choose an artificial high, but she's glad she didn't take that route. Her decisions in those keystone moments determined the life that she'd ultimately have.

Of all the messages I've heard about drugs and alcohol, Natural High's is the best one. It is powerful, convicting, and heartfelt.

While it breaks my heart that it evolved from tragedy, I'm thankful for Jon's courage and commitment to turn his pain into a purpose. Natural High's message has reached eight million students and forty-three thousand educators in fifty states.[3] What a legacy he has created.

Jon's mission matters because research shows that if middle schoolers choose not to consume drugs or alcohol, they're fourteen times less likely to ever become addicted. Also, nine out of ten addictions begin in the teenage years.[4] The right message at the right time can change their life trajectory.

Like Jon, your daughter has gifts and authentic life experiences that will help her serve others. She was created to wake up with a sense of purpose and devote her life to a greater cause. Even if she doesn't wake up with purpose now (like my daughters, she may need to be *dragged* out of bed), you can instill a mission mindset. All the deep questions she'll wrestle with in her lifetime—*Who am I? Why am I here? What is my purpose? Does my life matter?*—start to get answered as she sees herself as part of God's rescue plan to save mankind. God wants salvation for all. Every human plays a role in carrying out His will.

Knowing this invigorates your daughter's life with meaning. It helps her understand that her real home is in heaven, and life on earth is a pilgrimage to that sacred destination. Her greatest purpose is to know, love, and serve the Lord—and to do the best she can with each day she is given.

Living with a mission mindset helps your daughter do the following:

- **Think beyond herself.** "Love one another with brotherly affection. Outdo one another in showing honor" (Romans 12:10 ESV).
- **Devote her life to God.** "So whether you eat or drink or

whatever you do, do it all for the glory of God" (1 Corinthians 10:31 NIV).

- **Find joy in serving others.** "The greatest among you will be your servant. For those who exalt themselves will be humbled, and those who humble themselves will be exalted" (Matthew 23:11–12 NIV).

- **Dream big.** "God can do anything, you know—far more than you could ever imagine or guess or request in your wildest dreams! He does it not by pushing us around but by working within us, his Spirit deeply and gently within us" (Ephesians 3:20 MSG).

- **Stay humble.** "He must become greater and greater, and I must become less and less" (John 3:30).

- **Discover clarity and direction.** "Trust in the LORD with all your heart and lean not on your own understanding; in all your ways submit to him, and he will make your paths straight" (Proverbs 3:5–6 NIV).

- **Work hard and be generous.** "You know that these hands of mine have worked to supply my own needs and even the needs of those who were with me. And I have been a constant example of how you can help those in need by working hard. You should remember the words of the Lord Jesus: 'It is more blessed to give than to receive'" (Acts 20:34–35).

- **Resist pride and entitlement.** "The path of the virtuous leads away from evil; whoever follows that path is safe. Pride goes before destruction, and haughtiness before a fall" (Proverbs 16:17–18).

- **Build richer relationships.** "Walk with the wise and become wise; associate with fools and get in trouble" (Proverbs 13:20).

- **Feel deeply fulfilled.** "Take delight in the LORD, and he will give you the desires of your heart" (Psalm 37:4 NIV).
- **Come alive.** "For we are God's masterpiece. He has created us anew in Christ Jesus, so we can do the good things he planned for us long ago" (Ephesians 2:10).

Take a moment to ask yourself, *What are my daughter's natural giftings? What is her natural high?* Is it photography? Hiking? Wakeboarding? What motivates her, excites her, and makes her lose track of time? How can she inspire others and make them smile?

Your daughter is here to leave people better than she found them. Even quiet gifts—like knitting, baking, gardening, or painting—can bring tremendous joy to others while filling her heart with supernatural peace.

Like all of us, your daughter needs to feel needed. She isn't meant to wander aimlessly and idly pass the time. If she has a pulse, then she has a purpose. God has assignments for her.

Too many young people today turn to artificial highs. They use harmful substances to cope with anxiety, stress, pain, loneliness, depression, or hard life emotions. By helping your daughter tap into her natural high—and reminding her that her healthy passions will lead to her purpose—you show a better way. You point her toward a path that could save her life or someone else's.

Your daughter is never too young to do great things for God or to set an example for other believers (1 Timothy 4:12). If she helps just one person get to heaven by showing them Jesus, then her life is a success. By helping grow God's people, she grows His kingdom too.

> *If she helps just one person get to heaven by showing them Jesus, then her life is a success.*

129

What If Your Daughter Isn't on Fire for God?

Several years ago, a teenage girl messaged me through Instagram. She shared some recent highs and lows from her life. Then she asked me, "If I'm not on fire for God, is it really faith?"

For six months, she'd been on fire for the Lord, but now her passion was waning. She was practicing the spiritual disciplines (like reading her Bible and going to church), but her big feelings had stopped.

She now questioned her faith and wondered if it was ever real.

Unfortunately, our children have been shaped by a "go big or go home" culture. Even their faith journeys often feel defined by big feelings, big emotions, and big moments, especially as they watch viral videos of Christian celebrities who proclaim God's goodness on a stage or in a stadium.

It's wonderful to see believers enjoy mountaintop moments together. We need more supernatural moments that bring genuine worship and praise. But big moments can make small moments feel like failures in comparison. And when faith doesn't feel electric or intoxicating, many young people wonder if they're doing it wrong.

Many young people also depend on these highs to sustain their faith. They come home on fire for Jesus after a Christian conference, summer camp, or time with other believers, but as everyday life kicks back in, they get distracted and fall back into their old routine of putting faith on the back burner.

But like any life journey, pursuing God brings peaks and valleys. It includes cloud-nine moments and rock-bottom moments too. While mountaintop moments can ignite our faith, they can't sustain our faith. Real faith is often "a long obedience in the same direction."[5]

It takes maturity to stop living for big emotions. And it helps our daughters to know that spending time in the valleys of life is the ultimate test of faith.

Rick Warren said,

The most common mistake Christians make in worship today is seeking an *experience* rather than seeking God. They look for a feeling, and if it happens, they conclude that they have worshiped. Wrong! In fact, God often removes our feelings so we won't depend on them. Seeking a feeling, even the feeling of closeness to Christ, is not worship. When you are a baby Christian, God gives you a lot of confirming emotions and often answers to the most immature, self-centered prayers—so you'll know he exists. But as you grow in faith, he will wean you of these dependencies.[6]

In short, nobody is always on fire for God. Even the spiritual giants wrestled with doubt, disillusionment, and feeling deserted at times.

Mother Teresa, for instance, felt a deep sense of God's absence for most of her life. Through letters published after her death, we learn that her dark night of the soul lasted *fifty years*.[7] Only once did light pierce this darkness, and never again did she feel God's presence as clearly as she did while riding a train and hearing Jesus tell her to serve the poorest of the poor.

Despite this, Mother Teresa stayed faithful. She embraced God's plan for her life and kept things simple. She did small things with great love, giving her full attention to the person directly in front of her and treating them like the most important person on earth.

Over time, she deeply affected lives and widely impacted the world. She became a saint, a Nobel Peace Prize recipient, and one of *TIME* magazine's twenty-five most powerful women of the past century.[8] Mother Teresa never set out to be a worldwide sensation, yet that's what happened as she simply obeyed God.

God can work miracles with the smallest offering. He can turn two fish and five loaves into a feast for five thousand people (Matthew 14:17–19). Even if your daughter's faith is shaky, even when she feels like she has little to give, He can multiply each act of love.

Doing common things uncommonly well—like showing patience with her grandmother, writing thoughtful thank-you notes, helping a neighbor carry in groceries, noticing someone who is sitting alone—draws your daughter into a greater plan that can slowly transform her heart and the people around her.

Your daughter won't always feel like she's on fire for God. In some seasons, she may feel angry, run away, or experience a dark night of the soul. But rest assured that He never leaves her. He never stops loving her or pursuing her heart. When she can stand on this truth without needing proof that He is present, she'll know her faith is real. She'll see how she is becoming more than just a baby Christian.

Cultivate a Healthy Drive in Your Daughter

One key ingredient of living a purposeful life is having motivation. Without motivation, who wants to get out of bed? Who would ever leave home?

Motivation is the spark that gets us started. It prompts us to act on an urge or idea. But what keeps us going, even when the rewards end, is drive. And in the *Forbes* article "The Power of Drive: Why It Matters More Than Motivation and How to Cultivate It," author Ryan McGrath said that motivation can be a catalyst for change, but drive is what propels us forward toward a specific goal.

He shared this example:

> The marathon runner is highly motivated to run the race, but without the drive to train and persist through the physical and mental challenges ahead, they would struggle to achieve their goal. The drive to succeed is what pushes them to show up every day and train tirelessly, maintain a rigid diet and push through the discomfort of preparing for a 26.2-mile race. During training, there aren't any spectators, cheering friends or shiny trophies. This is when motivation dwindles and drive kicks in—when nobody is watching. Even if the race were to get rained out, a driven marathoner would likely still show up because they compete for personal fulfillment rather than external validation.[9]

As your daughter searches for purpose—and especially as she finds her purpose—encourage her to ask herself, *What is driving me? Why am I determined to achieve this goal? What is my why?*

Like anything in life, her drive can be healthy or unhealthy. It can be fueled by good intentions or misguided motives. A healthy drive comes from the Holy Spirit. It empowers her to do God's will.

Feeling determined to throw an amazing party for a friend who needs more joy in her life is an example of a healthy drive. Throwing this same party so she can show off or prove that she is an amazing friend is an example of an unhealthy drive. The action is the same, but the *why* is different.

Similarly, being driven by money, fame, power, appearances, or popularity won't satisfy your daughter's longing for purpose like the desire to please God. There is no substitute for the peace that comes when she's driven by eternal goals.

Here are talking points to share with your daughter to help her find her purpose:

1. **Your gifts are meant to lighten someone's load.** When you share them, you make their life easier. You unleash the power of community.

2. **Life isn't a competition. Nobody needs to lose their race so you can win yours.** Your calling is unique, so focus on what *you* were born to do while encouraging other girls in what *they* were born to do. In God's kingdom, there's room for everyone to thrive. Everyone contributes.

3. **To whom much is given, much is expected (Luke 12:48).** Your blessings are God's gift to you—and what you do with your blessings is your gift back. Give generously based on what you've received.

4. **You're here to make an eternal difference, not a temporary splash.** While some success has a short shelf life (like a fashion video that goes viral), other success is eternal (like teaching a child to read so they can learn the Bible). Know the difference so you can pursue the ultimate success.

5. **Your mission field can be anything.** It can be your lacrosse team, English class, workplace, sorority house, or favorite Starbucks shop. Ask yourself, *What weighs on my heart? What breaks my heart? What needs to change? What do*

I know that might help someone? Who could use a friend today? Whose day can I make? The answers will point you in the right direction.

6. **Volunteering grows your heart and your perspective.** Support organizations that you believe in, like a shelter for women and children or a ministry that brings fresh produce to low-income areas that don't have grocery stores.

7. **Every expert was once a beginner, so give yourself room to grow.** Take small steps of faith and ask God to guide you by revealing the next right thing to do.

8. **Your greatest contribution may be what you know.** Through technology, you can grow your faith quickly. You have more access to God's truth than any previous generation through apps, Bible studies, podcasts, and more. Just knowing the Lord qualifies you to help others by stirring their soul. As Dr. Tim Keller said, "Properly understood, Christianity is by no means the opiate of the people. It's more like the smelling salts."[10] The right word at the right time could be the smelling salts that someone needs. It could activate their faith journey.

In the Bible, Jesus' disciples received the gift of the Holy Spirit after He died. He promised earlier to send this advocate (John 16:7) to help them continue what He started. Strengthened and empowered by the Holy Spirit inside them, the disciples bravely preached the gospel. They grew the new church. They faced persecution and death, yet they didn't lose their drive or give up on the Great Commission to make disciples of all nations (Matthew 28:18–20).

This same Spirit that drove the disciples—and raised Jesus from the dead—is what God offers to you and your daughter.

Being energized and led by the Holy Spirit equips you to do astonishing things, far more than you can imagine.

> *Your daughter isn't here to perfect our world; she's here to improve it. She's called to bring heaven down to earth.*

Your daughter isn't here to perfect our world; she's here to improve it. She's called to bring heaven down to earth. Help her see why her life matters. Fan into flames the gifts that live inside her.

Show Up to Heaven Exhausted

Children are like arrows in the hands of a warrior (Psalm 127:4). And as parents, we decide where to aim the arrows. We love and shape our daughters for eighteen years, and then we send them into the future so God can use them beyond our time on earth.

Our highest goal is to raise Christ disciples. To help our daughters glorify God and invite others into this community of light. As belief in God hits historic lows,[11] this mission gains importance. So many young people search for hope apart from Christ, and through our daughters, we can speak to them.

One outstanding role model reaching the next generation is football legend Tim Tebow. With courage, joy, and clarity, Tim lives out his faith. And during a talk in my community, he said his deepest desire is to honor God and show up to heaven exhausted.

He explained:

> I hope I don't show up to heaven well rested. When we have the
> chance to run the race that is set before us; I want to show up to
> heaven exhausted from running, running towards my Savior,

towards the cross, towards hurting people, towards the gospel and believing that it was all worth it.[12]

May we *all* show up to heaven exhausted. May we hold nothing back when using our gifts, experiences, wisdom, and life stories to help others. Our daughters want to make us proud, and they'll run races inspired by what we praise. Do we celebrate their efforts to make an eternal difference? Do we look past grades, achievements, résumés, and material success?

Whether our daughters are arranging flowers for a bridal shower, connecting two friends who need to meet, donating to a fundraiser, teaching a cycle class, sharing their testimony about an eating disorder, turning their trauma into purpose, or giving back in another way, it's all worth celebrating. It all cultivates a spirit of generosity that brings them fully alive.

Packing purpose in your daughter's suitcase is essential because it generates momentum. It lays the groundwork for a meaningful—and deeply rewarding—life. She longs to know that her life matters. She thrives when she feels needed. As your daughter makes contributions and sees the impact, her confidence grows. She becomes a kingdom builder.

Truths Worth Packing

- "Do not despise these small beginnings, for the LORD rejoices to see the work begin." (Zechariah 4:10)
- "You can make many plans, but the LORD's purpose will prevail." (Proverbs 19:21)
- "Therefore, go and make disciples of all the nations, baptizing them in the name of the Father and the Son and the Holy Spirit. Teach these new disciples to obey all the commands I have given you. And be sure of this: I am with you always, even to the end of the age." (Matthew 28:19–20)
- "As for me, my life has already been poured out as an offering to God. The time of my death is near. I have fought the good fight, I have finished the race, and I have remained faithful." (2 Timothy 4:6–7)
- "If you keep quiet at a time like this, deliverance and relief for the Jews will arise from some other place, but you and your relatives will die. Who knows if perhaps you were made queen for just such a time as this?" (Esther 4:14)

Questions to Unpack

1. What is your daughter's natural high? When did you first notice it?
2. What unique life experiences has your daughter had? How might God use her story to bring heaven down to earth?

3. What is your daughter's greatest place of impact? Where does her purpose play out most clearly right now?

A Prayer to Lighten Your Load

Dear Lord,
Help my daughter be wise with her time, energy, and talent. Break her heart for what breaks Yours. Inspire dreams driven by the Holy Spirit, and keep her humble when she succeeds. I praise You for the hidden gifts and capabilities planted inside her heart. Inspire her to seek Your will. In Jesus' name I pray, amen.

CHAPTER 9

PERSEVERANCE

CELEBRATE RESILIENCE

You can never have a comeback without a
setback. It's literally impossible. So when we
do face setbacks in our lives, we may not be
comfortable, we may not be satisfied, but
we can choose in those moments to have the
mindset: "I'm gonna have a crazy comeback."

TIM TEBOW

A ninth-grade girl didn't make the volleyball team, and she was devastated. As one of the best members of the team, her elimination made no sense. Everyone was shocked.

Her parents loved to watch her play. They never missed a game, and they found a home for themselves sitting in the stands with other parents. This sport brought their family tremendous joy. Her parents were heartbroken for her and sad for themselves.

It hurt them to see their daughter devastated and confused about this rejection.

It was a long night of tears, emotions, and good friends texting the family to express their sadness too.

Shortly after the news broke, this girl spoke to her best friend. They cried together because they loved being teammates. Volleyball was their shared passion, and now it wouldn't be the same for either of them. "I can't believe it," the heartbroken girl told her friend. "But what makes it even worse is that every time I go into the den, I see my parents crying and staring at each other, just shaking their heads. I feel like I've disappointed them."

I know this girl's parents, and they are amazing. I can say with certainty they were *not* disappointed in their daughter. They were simply sad and thrown for a loop because she deserved to make the cut.

But what we *know* in our hearts and what our daughters *perceive* as they observe us can be two different things. For a fifteen-year-old girl, seeing both her parents fall apart added to her heartache. Besides feeling crushed, she now felt guilty. Guilty for causing distress and making them sad.

What we know in our hearts and what our daughters perceive as they observe us can be two different things.

Let me clarify here that good parents show compassion. Good parents empathize when their child is upset. They comfort them, grieve, and often cry too. To simply dismiss our children's heartache or tell them to get over it would be heartless and cruel. It would deter them from ever coming to us again with a future heartache.

Yet when your daughter's heart is broken and she needs comfort from you, it's crucial to remember this: There is a distinction between grieving *with* hope and grieving *without* hope. Our job as parents is to keep hope in the picture. Our girls look to us for clues on how to respond to pain, and they crave reassurance that today's pain will end. Things will get better, and their heavy emotions won't last forever.

Grieving with hope comes from 1 Thessalonians 4:13–14, which says when you grieve, don't grieve like those who have no hope. A believer who mourns the death of another believer can grieve with hope because they know that person is with Jesus.

A priest shared this message at my father-in-law's funeral, and since then I've often thought: If this is true in *death*, isn't it equally true in our earthly trials? No darkness lasts forever, and with Jesus the best is yet to come.

What this fifteen-year-old girl taught me is to save my biggest reactions for behind closed doors. If I need to fall apart, it's best to do so privately (with my husband, in my car, in the shower, etc.), and not in front of my daughter. This helps me stay strong for her. It lets me deal honestly with my emotions without sending a message to my daughter that we can't handle her trials. Because if I can't handle her disappointments, how will she handle them? How will she have a crazy comeback if I only see the setback?

As moms, we like to beat ourselves up. I often hear narratives like this:

> My daughter is struggling, especially with friendships. I feel like I've failed her, like I didn't parent her personality right or set her up to handle adversity. She's going to college soon, and I'm running out of time to help her become her best self. I'm worried that I did it all wrong.

Can our mistakes as parents contribute to the struggles our daughters face? Of course. But we can't take all the blame, and we don't have to lose all hope. As Adam Grant said, "The purpose of reviewing your mistakes isn't to shame your past self. It's to educate your future self."[1] Once you know better, you can do better. You can create a brighter tomorrow.

Even if you could parent perfectly, you can't save your daughter from every heartache. You can't circumvent every rejection. There are no shortcuts to maturity, and part of your parenting journey is learning to trust the process when her life turns upside down.

It's crushing to witness your daughter's pain, yet there is also a blessing when it happens under your roof. It's a chance to coach her in recovery skills and celebrate her resilience. Once your daughter is in a calmer place, maybe a few days or a few weeks after the rejection, you can ask her, "What will your recovery be? How will you respond to this setback?"

A father of five teenagers came up with this phrase, and I love how it sets a hopeful tone. It tells your child, "You're going to make mistakes, and hard things will happen. So how will you respond when things don't go as planned? How will you make the best of a bad situation? What choices can move you in the right direction?"

When my daughters faced heartaches under my roof, I remembered what I once heard a counselor say: In college, one of the most at-risk groups are the high school superstars who have never experienced failure. For the first time ever—away from their parents, home, and lifelong support system—they experience a major trial. Without a road map to navigate this experience, they feel lost. It doesn't always go well when they lack the skills to cope.

Even if your daughter chooses work, vocational school, or

another path into the real world, this same principle applies. Feeling surrounded by love, comfort, and the familiarity of home softens the blow of heartache. What Dr. Tim Keller said about marriage—"Marriage provides a profound 'shock absorber' that helps you navigate disappointments, illnesses, and other difficulties. You recover your equilibrium faster"[2]—holds true in other key relationships too.

Through this lens, your daughter's trials become opportunities to learn about perseverance. They become teachable moments at home that prepare her for bigger trials. Through your support, she can recover her equilibrium faster. She can feel hope for what is ahead and build more endurance.

Heartache may be part of your daughter's story, but it's not the end of her story. If it's not good, then God's not done. Her story is still being written, and with you by her side to celebrate her resilience, she can make a comeback.

Even after a major disappointment, you can grieve with hope. You can encourage your daughter to take baby steps forward. There's always something to celebrate as she works toward a goal. No trial is bigger than God's plan for her and the tenacity inside her heart.

Do You Ever Call the Game at Halftime?

My husband and I love to watch college football, and we root for our alma mater. Watching these young athletes persevere—and stay in a hard-fought game—always inspires me. On a national stage, they teach lessons in resilience.

As parents, we often hear, "You don't call the game at halftime. You don't give up when things look bad." Yet sometimes, we do this. We feel tempted to throw in the towel as we believe our child's future is doomed by the odds stacked against them.

Whether it's a health crisis, a huge mistake, a rejection, a betrayal, a mean girl situation, a breakup, a broken promise, a scandal, an injury, a public humiliation, or another trial, we can get so weighed down by our daughter's current circumstances that we lose hope for the future.

We can lose sight of God's ability to write an incredible comeback story.

But our girls deserve a better outlook. They have enough naysayers, pessimists, and critics speaking into their lives already, and they need more voices of hope. They need us to believe they can bounce back and prove their critics wrong.

Just like athletes who fight until the clock runs out, our daughters need resilience. They need a mental toughness that keeps them engaged in life and positioned to achieve big goals.

Many teams have enjoyed amazing comeback stories. And one story I'll never forget, as a lifelong Alabama fan, played out at the 2018 College Football Playoff National Championship.

Throughout the first half, Alabama struggled. Georgia dominated the game, and by halftime, Georgia had a 13–0 lead. The high hopes I felt walking into that stadium seemed like a distant memory.

But in the second half, the momentum shifted. Coach Nick Saban replaced starting quarterback Jalen Hurts with a new quarterback named Tua Tagovailoa. Tua put Bama back in the game. His talent was unbelievable, yet nobody had seen his skills since he didn't play much during the season. Little did we know, the team had a secret weapon.

Alabama bounced back, but Georgia fought hard, too, and the

game became an emotional roller coaster. With four minutes left on the scoreboard, Alabama was seven points behind. A victory felt close . . . yet still impossible.

Several of our Bama friends left the stadium early. They couldn't take the beatdown. I considered leaving, too, but we opted to stay. I'll always be thankful for that decision because what happened next was one of the greatest thrills I've ever witnessed. In my thirty years with Harry, through dating and marriage, we agree this ranks as a top-ten memory for us.

Alabama rallied and tied the game. It went into overtime—and I still get chills when I think about Tua's forty-one-yard pass to DeVonta Smith in the end zone that won the game at the last minute and made them both legends. It was an epic comeback by two true freshmen.

This game was the ultimate tale of two halves. We never could have predicted the second half based on the first half.

And the truth is, *many* games are won in the last few seconds. Many players who get benched, like Jalen Hurts after this championship, use their season of waiting to get stronger and better. Jalen went on to achieve outstanding success in the NFL (and led his team to a Super Bowl victory in 2024!), and Georgia enjoyed its own comeback by later winning two national championships, including one win against Alabama. College football is never short of surprises.

And honestly, parenting isn't either. If miracles can happen in a football game, how much more might God do in your daughter's life? How sad would you be if you checked out early and missed her amazing comeback?

You can't judge your daughter's future by her current circumstances. At her age, a lot can change in three weeks, three months, or three years. The girl who gets bullied and loses confidence in middle school can slowly regain confidence as she finds her footing in creative arts. By the time she graduates, she may be editor of the yearbook, have a thriving photography business, or be crushing it as a graphic designer. Her turnaround might come after transferring to a school with a better culture or homeschooling for a year to rebuild her sense of worth.

The key for us, as moms, is to be patient and prayerful. What is best for your daughter may look different from what is best for her friends or her siblings. Just recently I visited a community where some families send their kids to three different school systems. Every grade at every school has its own dynamic, and while some kids do fine at the large public school, others get eaten alive. They need a smaller setting to feel comfortable being themselves.

When our girls are little, they need a cop. When they're teenagers, they need a coach. As they leave home, they need a consultant.

As our girls grow up, our role changes. When our girls are little, they need a cop. When they're teenagers, they need a coach. As they leave home, they need a consultant.

Right now, most of us are in coaching mode or preparing for it. We're evaluating the playing field and all the social, academic, and psychological dynamics that our daughters will need to navigate. We're preparing them for scenarios they haven't faced yet. We're coaching them through disappointments and sending them back out on the field. We're noticing their potential, building their strengths, and challenging them to rise and become the best version of themselves.

We have good days and bad days, victories and defeats, but what we don't do is call the game at halftime. Instead, we hang in there, believe in our child, and consult God as *our* coach as we coach our daughters.

Your daughter's place of struggle can lead to an amazing comeback story. God often shows up in the very places where you worry about your child getting left behind.

One of my daughters, for instance, struggled with math. It never came naturally to her like it did her sisters, who signed up for the hardest classes. Throughout elementary school, she needed tutors and extra help. Her teachers kept her in early intervention. I often told her how lucky she was to have teachers who cared and helped her catch up. She adored these teachers and loved the extra support. I felt grateful—yet also worried deep down that middle school math would break her confidence. I worried about her failing and feeling dumb.

Yet here's what happened: Her struggle created an amazing work ethic. Her first middle school math teacher sang her praises because she always paid attention and stayed engaged. For two years, she won the math award for her entire grade. Her teachers tried to convince her to take advanced math, but she stuck with the regular track.

When I emailed her first middle school math teacher to thank her for everything, she replied, "She is so sweet and so smart! I LOVE that she asks questions in class because not only does it help her, but it also helps the other students. I am so lucky to have her!"

My daughter will never be a math genius, but her growth in this subject makes me so proud. This victory might seem small to you, but to me, it's everything. I know the backstory that led to this win. I have that special "in."

You have that special "in" with your daughter too. As the keeper of her life story, you can celebrate her resilience on a micro level. Your daughter needs an encouraging coach because the world will define her by her stumbles and defeats. She needs your positive outlook and willingness to pivot when a strategy isn't working.

Your daughter's childhood can be a tale of two halves. Teaching her to learn from the past, anticipate the future, and make timely adjustments helps keep her in the game of life.

Even if she makes a big mistake—like becoming a mean girl and losing her friends—there is hope. She's not destined for permanent solitude. Instead, you can help her change. You can help her write an incredible comeback story with these steps:

- Step one: Love her as she faces the fallout.
- Step two: Help her admit her mistakes.
- Step three: Encourage her to apologize to the people she hurt.
- Step four: Remind her to be patient as she starts at ground zero to rebuild trust.
- Step five: Keep praying and praising God in advance for His good plan for her.

Your proudest parenting moments may come in the second half of a hard season. Your daughter can't grow backward, so focus on moving forward. Imagine what can be. The mean girl fallout may lead to a moment two years later where you celebrate your daughter's birthday and try not to cry as she is surrounded by great friends who love her. You may thank God for this turn of events as they cheerfully sing to her.

Great coaching and smart pivots can help your daughter recover. They can stimulate victories you never saw coming. Don't wave the white flag, call the game at halftime, or give up with four minutes left on the clock. Instead, believe in God as a waymaker and a miracle worker. Look for His hand in your daughter's comeback story.

Tell Your Daughter, "God Made You Strong"

When Corrie ten Boom was a young girl, she experienced a gripping fear of her loved ones dying after visiting a young mom whose baby died. Seeing the baby in its crib made death a reality.

That night, as Corrie's father tucked her into bed, she burst into tears. "I need you," Corrie told him. "You can't die! You can't!"

Her father sat on the edge of her narrow bed. He gently said, "Corrie . . . when you and I go to Amsterdam—when do I give you your ticket?"

"Why, just before we get on the train," Corrie replied.

"Exactly. And our wise Father in heaven knows when we are going to need things, too. Don't run out ahead of Him, Corrie. When the time comes that some of us will have to die, you will look into your heart and find the strength you need—just in time."[3]

God's grace comes when you need it most, and not a moment sooner. If you're gripped by the fear of a potential crisis next Saturday, it's because God hasn't delivered the grace you'll need for next Saturday yet.

We need this reminder, don't we? Grace meets us exactly where we are—but it doesn't leave us there. Instead, it changes us. It transforms us from the inside out.

We all have dreams for our daughters that sometimes get dashed. Unexpected plot twists upend our plans. This could look like the boy your daughter planned to marry calling it off with her to marry someone else. It could look like your very athletic daughter, recruited to run track by five Division I colleges, losing every option as a foot injury changes her speed. It could look like the trauma of losing someone she loves.

After a major heartache, we all need time to grieve. We need the space and grace to get our bearings and figure out the next step. For the benefit of your daughter (and yourself), do whatever it takes to stay healthy, rested, and sane. Invest in a solid counselor, exercise, clear your calendar, and say no to anything nonessential. This isn't the time to feel guilty or juggle too many balls. It's the time to prioritize your daughter's wellness and your wellness too.

Resilient moms build resilient girls. The stronger and more stable you are, the more effective you'll be in boosting her confidence.

You don't have to be an expert. You aren't meant to be her savior. But you can work wonders by increasing her sense of capability—and reminding her that one day, she'll share her story of survival to help someone else survive their trial. She'll tell her children and grandchildren about what she overcame to inspire hope in their disappointments.

What looks like a very dark place, a place where your daughter's been buried, could also be a place where she has been planted for new growth. Even in the darkest soil, she is designed to keep pushing forward. She has the ability to dig deep and rise. As grief counselor Farrell Mason said, "We were made to resurrect."[4]

Here are words to encourage your daughter when she is down on her luck.

- "God made you strong. I believe in you, and I'm excited to see what happens from here."
- "You're doing the best you can in a situation that's far from ideal. I'm proud of you."

- "I may not always love your choices, but I'll always love you."
- "Don't let a waiting season be a wasted season. What happens to you while you're waiting is often more important than what you're waiting for."
- "Failure isn't fatal. In fact, it's often the birthplace of success."
- "You may have a wild ride, but you'll land on your feet. You'll be okay!"
- "You're surviving what you thought you couldn't. The sky is the limit from here."
- "Turn the page. Your comeback story starts now."

Resilience isn't always pretty. Resurrection won't happen overnight. But as your daughter taps into her inner strength, she sets the stage for growth. She learns the art of bouncing back.

Help her become someone she feels proud of. Celebrate her courage as she does hard things. Staying *resilient* in setbacks and *humble* in comebacks keeps her in the game of life. It cultivates a spirit that may be her secret weapon.

Love Your Daughter Through Her Battles

I love watching Jenna Bush Hager on the *TODAY* show. I've had a soft spot for Jenna ever since she made headlines in college after her dad became president of the United States—and she was caught for underage drinking and trying to buy alcohol.

Looking back, she said, "The best gift we can give our children . . . is the chance to fail. While we were growing up, I for one had parents that let us fail, let us fall and publicly. And I always say to them now, 'How brave of you,' because it didn't reflect great on them, either."

Jenna's phone call confession to her dad after being caught was a lesson in humility and how to handle a child's transgression. She embarrassed him on a national stage, yet he never said that. He never called her out for bringing shame to the family. He also didn't let her take all the blame. When she said she was sorry, he said he was sorry too. He'd told her she could be normal even though he was the president, but she couldn't be.[5]

Publicly or not, our daughters will face embarrassments, setbacks, heartaches, and hard consequences. They'll make some decisions that call into question how well we've done our job.

If your first reaction is, *How does this reflect on me? What will people think?* then something is wrong. You may be putting your image, your ego, or your pride above your daughter's well-being. You may be making your daughter's problem all about *you*. This leaves you ill-equipped to help. It makes you an outsider in her comeback story.

One necessity in building a child's resilience is having at least one strong relationship with a loving adult. Even after childhood trauma, the kids who adapt and overcome adversity best have at least one stable, committed, and supportive adult relationship. These relationships build a resilience that turn "toxic stress into tolerable stress."[6]

Your daughter doesn't need an entourage or a huge friend group to survive her darkest days. Clearly, friends matter, but your presence in her time of pain matters even more. After all, you *live* with her. You know how well she is eating, sleeping, thinking, and functioning. You pick up on changes in her mood, behavior, and personality. You have a mother's intuition and a passion to see her thrive. You'd walk through fire for her, and you care about her well-being unlike anyone else in the world. So don't discount your impact. Don't dismiss the significance of showing her extra love as she recovers from a defeat.

Even a small act of love—like having her favorite Greek salad waiting for her after school, putting a funny card and new pajamas on her bed, letting her chores slide for the week, adding fresh flowers in her bathroom, taking her and a friend to get a manicure, decorating the inside of her car with balloons—could go a long way in brightening her day.

One day when you're gone, your daughter will face trials without you. She won't have your voice in her ear or your acts of love. She'll yearn for your presence, but the good news is, she may hear your voice and know *exactly* what to do based on your prior responses. She may have a blueprint of how to persevere after years of watching you.

Who your daughter is becoming today matters more than who she's been in the past. Life may disappoint her, but it doesn't have to break her. It can't keep her from finishing the good work God has started in her life story.

Packing perseverance in your daughter's suitcase is essential because she'll need endurance for her life journey. You can't fight her battles for her, but you can love her through them. You can ride out the storms and celebrate her resilience. When all is said and done, some of your proudest parenting moments may come from watching your daughter bounce back. You'll be glad you hung in there and refused to call the game at halftime.

Truths Worth Packing

- "God is within her, she will not fall; God will help her at break of day." (Psalm 46:5 NIV)
- "Consider it pure joy, my brothers and sisters, whenever you face trials of many kinds, because you know that the testing of your faith produces perseverance. Let perseverance finish its work so that you may be mature and complete, not lacking anything." (James 1:2–4 NIV)
- "May our daughters be like graceful pillars, carved to beautify a palace." (Psalm 144:12)
- "A woman giving birth to a child has pain because her time has come; but when her baby is born she forgets the anguish because of her joy that a child is born into the world. So with you: Now is your time of grief, but I will see you again and you will rejoice, and no one will take away your joy." (John 16:21–22 NIV)
- "Do not gloat over me, my enemy! Though I have fallen, I will rise. Though I sit in darkness, the LORD will be my light." (Micah 7:8 NIV)

Questions to Unpack

1. Have you ever waved the white flag in parenting? Looking back, what made you feel hopeless? What lies fed your sense of defeat?
2. Name a time when your daughter showed impressive resilience. Have you ever told her? If not, do it today!

3. If you reflect on your darkest days, you may realize that it wasn't ten people who became your saving grace. Most likely, it was one or two key people (your mom, your dad, your grandmother, your track coach). Who has influenced your daughter like this? Who else builds her resilience?

A Prayer to Lighten Your Load

Dear Lord,
Carry my daughter through her trials. Be the anchor that steadies her. Cultivate resilience, fortitude, and mental toughness. Create new blessings in times of pain. I praise You for being steadfast, even in uncertainty. Bless my daughter with the stamina to endure suffering and rise again. Strengthen me as I journey beside her. In Jesus' name I pray, amen.

CHAPTER 10

FAITH

TRUST GOD

As a parent, I can find peace with not being able
to protect my children in everything. While it
pains me to know that my children will experience
the harsh and sour world more than I'd ever want
them to, I know that it is God's way of revealing
the incredibly soft and sweet contrast of the gospel.

LAURA WIFLER

My friend's daughter, Emily, kept a journal for her future husband.

Long before Emily met him, she prayed for him and wrote down prayers. For years her journal entries grew—until one day she finally met Luke.

A few weeks before their wedding, Emily shared this journal with Luke. She gave it to him as a gift. What jumped out as her fiancé read through it was a passage from the Bible that Emily had prayed years earlier in one specific season. It was a chapter that God placed on her heart: Isaiah 49. It's a long poem that isn't commonly heard or shared. Here is an excerpt:

> Shout for joy, you heavens;
> rejoice, you earth;
> burst into song, you mountains!
> For the LORD comforts his people
> and will have compassion on his afflicted ones.
>
>   (v. 13 NIV)

Unbeknownst to Emily, at this exact time in Luke's life, he was reeling from a difficult breakup. He was heartbroken, and as his father comforted him, he gave Luke a promise from God to cling to. *It was the same passage from Isaiah that his future wife was praying for him from many miles away. The passage that God placed on Emily's heart.*

While some people may call this a coincidence, I call it a God wink.[1] I consider it evidence that He cares about the details of our children's lives and is always orchestrating yet-to-be-revealed blessings behind the scenes.

At Luke and Emily's wedding, an overwhelming warmth filled the church. The Holy Spirit was present, and watching this couple take their vows felt undeniably *good*. Every guest walked out of that church smiling and feeling uplifted. Joy was in the air, and when a wedding has that effect—a palpable joy that can't be manufactured or forced—you know it's from God. It's a foreshadowing of the perfect joy we'll experience in heaven.

We can't see it, but the Lord is always a step ahead. He's setting the stage for your daughter's future using events that happen today. He walks with her *and* before her, never leaving her side so that she won't feel discouraged or afraid (Deuteronomy 31:8).

What feels insignificant, random, or even devastating could be a primary thread being woven into a bigger story. As American playwright and author Thornton Wilder once wrote (and Harold Kushner discussed in his book *When Bad Things Happen to Good People*), life is like a tapestry. As humans, we mostly see the back side. We see a hodgepodge of many threads—loose ends, knots, and random patterns. But God sees the front. From His vantage point, the threads of arbitrary events can ultimately coincide to form a beautiful work of art. Every twist and knot has its place in a great design.[2] It's all intricately woven together.

On this side of heaven, there will always be mysteries we don't understand, loose ends we can't comprehend. While some events will come full circle and make more sense down the road, there will also be suffering that feels pointless, heartless, and cruel— devastation that we can't mitigate with a tapestry analogy.

Our deepest heartaches present a crossroads. They force us to make a choice: to trust God or reject Him. Faith means trusting the Lord before we have all the answers. It takes courage to trust God's plan for your life—and even more courage to trust God's plan for your daughter.

Especially when she's hurting and you're praying desperate prayers, waiting on the Lord to act may be the hardest thing you do. It could lead to a crisis of faith.

It helps me to remember that God loves my children far more than I do. He knows every detail about their future. When I feel tempted to control loose ends—and frustrated by unanswered questions—I remind myself to keep trusting Him. My job is to enable, not interrupt, His plan.

The Lord works all things together for good for those who love Him (Romans 8:28). He weaves every seemingly random thread into an intricate tapestry. Learning to trust God with your daughter's life story teaches her to do the same. Beyond the heartache and brokenness of today is a future that only He can see.

Is Control Your Idol?

Some mornings when I wake up, my hands are sore from clenching my fists. It's embarrassing to admit this, but it happens as I sleep. I'm anxious by nature, and even as I work on being calmer, I carry unconscious fears and worries.

Especially as my girls grow up and spread out to four different places, the physical distance and lack of control can get to me. Call it what you want—maybe a false sense of security—but I sleep best when all my babies are together at home, safe and sound under my roof. In these moments, I feel like all is right with the world. I can fully relax.

Parenting older kids means accepting the discomfort of releasing them to God. Being a "praying mom" takes on a whole new meaning as our daughters become young adults.

In many ways, I love this current season where my girls are ages fifteen, eighteen, twenty, and twenty-two. I don't long to go back to having four little ones under the age of seven because that season was exceptionally hard for me. I prefer my big kids and the deeper relationships we have now.

At the same time, my worries grow as they leave home. Bigger fears about tomorrow—and what the real world may bring—can steal my joy today.

When I feel paralyzed, I know it's time for a reset. It's my reminder to breathe and remember God's faithfulness in my life and throughout history. I'm prone to make control my idol, and like many moms, I often soothe my anxiety by trying to smooth the way.

I struggle to find the balance between doing my job as a mom and trusting God with my daughters' lives. After all, motherhood calls for action. We're called to love, guide, and protect our children, and our children are called to actively participate in their own lives. "Trusting God" doesn't mean that we become passive, lazy, or apathetic. It's not an excuse to sit back and wait for blessings to pour down.

But the key, I believe, is to work in tandem with God. To teach our daughters to do their best—and then leave the results to Him. God can weave any outcome into a greater story. Nothing is a waste if it builds your daughter's character and faith.

If she longs to win a swimming award, encourage her to work hard to earn it, but don't call in favors so she gets it.

If she struggles in geometry, get her the extra help she needs, but don't do her homework for her.

If she doesn't win the student election, let her grieve and be sad, but don't make them recount votes, blame the administration, or speak poorly of the winner.

As I said earlier, our daughters take their cues from us. Our responses affect their responses. As we trust God, they learn to trust Him too. You'll know you're doing something right when your daughter's response to her own heartache is more mature than yours. It's funny to see the tables turn!

A Texas mom once told me about a twenty-four-hour rule in her daughter's theatre troupe. After a big announcement, like casting choices for a new play, you can't talk about your role outside your family for one day. You can't chat with friends, post on social media, or complain to the director.

This mom admitted how this rule has saved her many times. After one announcement, she was furious. She wanted to withdraw her daughter after she was placed in the ensemble *again*. But her daughter loves to act, and she knew quitting would prevent her from ever getting the lead. She begged her mom not to complain. She talked her mom off the ledge.

The next day, when this mom had calmed down, she saw the situation differently. She was thankful for her daughter's counsel that stopped her from expressing outrage. With a little time, she was able to laugh at herself and the irony of their role reversal.

Our daughters won't always get what they want or deserve. Our plans won't always manifest the way we hope and dream. But before we cause a scene or try to manipulate a new outcome, let's remember that God works in all circumstances. We don't have to fear a broken heart because a broken heart is an open heart. It may be the catalyst that drives our daughters to Him.

Your daughter won't know God's comfort until her heart aches with disappointment.

She won't believe a friend can drop her until a friendship suddenly ends.

She won't discover that faith is a powerful anchor until all other comforts are gone.

Most importantly, she won't understand that Jesus is all she needs until Jesus is all she has.

What starts as a shock or a sudden change in plans can be a chance for your daughter to start over. It can inspire her to rebuild her life with Jesus as her rock. On this foundation, she'll still be standing when circumstances change. She'll survive heartaches and understand why God wants to be her number one: Because her heart was made to worship, and when He's not her number one, she'll take a good thing (like a friendship, a romance, or the lead role in the play) and make it the ultimate thing. In other words, she'll worship the wrong god.

Rejection happens to all of us, and even Jesus felt it. The stone that the builders rejected eventually became the cornerstone (Matthew 21:42). What feels like a life-changing event—your daughter's broken heart—could actually be the starting point for renewed confidence and faith.

It could eventually become a primary thread in her life story.

Our daughters have a Savior, but that savior isn't us. We have less power and control than we think. Parenting with clenched fists leads to a singular vision of how your daughter's life should look. Anything less than plan A doesn't feel good enough. Anything less than plan A is considered a failure.

> Our daughters have a Savior, but that savior isn't us.

But far more prolific than your vision for your daughter is God's vision for her. Parenting with open palms, rather than clenched fists, keeps you flexible and ready to adapt. It frees your daughter from your expectations and allows you both to notice God's hand in her journey—and what new doors He may have opened.

Be a Praying Mom

I meet a lot of people in ministry who used to be the "wild child."

Over time, I've noticed two common denominators: (1) They're always humble, and (2) they know how to reach the hard-to-reach people. They speak effectively to those on the margins of faith. They have a heart for lost souls because they were once *them*. These former renegades are proof that nobody is a lost cause. Even those with a checkered past can do enormous good once they give their heart to God.

Many parents today wrestle with a prodigal child. Their hearts are weary, and their faith is tested. Believing God is trustworthy gets complicated when your prayers go unanswered or when your child keeps rejecting Him.

But remember: He is a God of miracles. He never forgets about your child. Nothing can make God stop loving your daughter or pursuing her heart.

The story of Saint Augustine is one of my favorite inspirations. Raised in the Christian faith, he rebelled as a teenager. For seventeen years, his mother prayed. She cried many tears over her wayward son and his lifestyle.

Augustine returned to the faith in his early thirties. He spent the rest of his life serving God in history-making ways.

Today Saint Augustine is known as one of the greatest saints of all times. It's been 1,600 years since his death, yet more than five million words of his writings still exist in print.[3] You can order his books on Amazon, which feels absolutely crazy to me. That's like this book still being published in 3625!

Augustine's mom, Saint Monica, was a prayer warrior. Can you imagine praying the same prayer for *seventeen years*? I'm afraid I'd give up, but thankfully, she didn't. Without Saint Monica, we might not have Saint Augustine. He couldn't outrun his mother's prayers, and thanks to her, we have a hero of faith who finished strong despite a rocky start.

Like all of us, your daughter is a work in progress. Who she is today isn't who she will be in five, ten, or twenty years. Her faith and character are still forming, and if they're not as advanced as you hoped, it's okay. God still loves her wildly. He always welcomes her back.

What your daughter knows in her *head* may not connect to her *heart*. She may think that God wants to spoil her fun. She may struggle to believe she's worthy or good enough to be loved by Him. She may wrestle with problems that shake her faith. She may doubt that He even exists.

Whatever limits or blocks her faith, pray for her. Pray for open eyes and a heart on fire for Jesus. Pray for God to overwhelm her with His supernatural presence. Pray for her to finish strong in her life journey and influence lives even after she's gone.

Faith is a spiritual gift that comes more naturally to some than others. Whether your daughter's faith is strong already or has a lot of room to grow, being her prayer warrior matters. Don't lose sight of what God can do in the home—and the heart—of a praying mom. Don't underestimate the impact of prayers that your daughter can't outrun.

"Fear Not" the Future

I love being a mother, and I feel passionate about encouraging other mothers in their journey.

That's why it saddens me to hear that global birth rates have plummeted. America's birth rate is the lowest it's been in forty years. It's fallen for the past fifteen years—yet the number of women in their prime childbearing years has risen over 9 percent.[4]

Many factors influence this. But one common reason I hear from young couples is that our world isn't safe. Who in their right mind would bring a baby here? Why would we subject innocent children to the potential perils of this world?

Honestly, I understand the hesitation. I can't blame anyone for thinking twice. As a young bride, I turned on the news one morning and saw that America had been attacked by terrorists on 9/11. Harry and I were trying to get pregnant at the time and had just experienced a miscarriage. That pregnancy only lasted three days, yet it ignited in me an overwhelming desire to have a child.

As I watched the news unfold, I felt very afraid. I suddenly doubted our decision and wondered if having a baby would be a big mistake. It felt safer not to take a chance, to take the topic of children off the table forever. But in the weeks that followed, our desire for a baby grew bigger than our fears. We longed to be parents, so we took a leap of faith and welcomed our first child the next September.

Since then, she and her three sisters have brought us unspeakable joy. They've elevated our lives to an entirely new league of meaning and joy. By God's grace we took a chance, and I'm forever grateful we did. It pains me to think about what we may have missed.

Before our children are even born, fear can dominate our parenting decisions. Fear can convince us that evil is bigger than God.

One of God's most frequent demands in the Bible is "Fear not." He knows we need constant reminding that He is always with us, and we don't have to fear the future because Jesus promises eternal life. When we walk with Him, we're secure. We can stand on His promises.

Yet the darkness of doubt is real, and one of Satan's favorite tricks is to undermine our trust in God. Dark times make us vulnerable to believing his lies, and that's when we need the truth most. What we learn in the light, we'll use in the dark. A flashlight of faith becomes our saving grace.

God wants us to be fruitful and multiply (Genesis 1:28; 9:7). Raising children who love the Lord—and bring others to the Lord—is part of His master plan. As we grow a faithful family, we grow God's family too. We help push back the darkness.

It takes courage to raise a child today. It's easy to become jaded and discourage new life, but I like Jonathan Pokluda's perspective. It reminds me of what we're preparing our daughters for.

He said: "If you say, 'Well, the world is too corrupt,' I'd say, 'Well, what if your child is the solution? . . . What if the cure for the corruption of the world is the child that you're supposed to have and raise?'"[5]

What a powerful framework. What a thought-provoking mental pivot from feeling hopeless and afraid.

What if God brought your daughter and my daughters into existence as *solutions* to our fallen world?

What if they've been specifically designed to live in this era?

What if we're not just raising children—but also raising future women, wives, mothers, and leaders who will spread out far and wide, planting themselves in different communities as unified forces for good?

What if our daughters fight the darkness because we prepared them for it? What if their faith wakes up their generation?

What if their trials lead to someone's salvation?

What if God has deliberately crossed our paths? What if the timing of you reading this book feels providential, not accidental?

What if your greatest accomplishment is who you help your daughter become?

What if a tiny dream in your heart is actually meant for your daughter? What if God's plan for her builds on your faithfulness?

In Scripture, King David dreamed of building a temple for God. God told him this desire was good, but David wouldn't be the one to do this. God chose Solomon, David's son, to build that temple instead. Solomon would continue his father's dynasty (2 Chronicles 6:7–9).

Sometimes God gives you a vision . . . but not the plan. He offers a prelude of what's to come. I can't speak for David, but I'd be thrilled if God chose my child to carry out a dream that started in my heart. That plan is even better because we want our girls to outdo us. We want them to stand on our spiritual shoulders.

> *We want our girls to outdo us. We want them to stand on our spiritual shoulders.*

There will always be reasons to live in fear, but perfect love casts out fear (1 John 4:18). Perfect love awakens hope. God is good, and His plan for your daughter is worth the wait. You don't have to carry the world on your shoulders, because the future is safe in His hands. Let go of what you can't control so you can love, champion, and prepare your daughter for life beyond your home.

Packing faith in your daughter's suitcase is essential because the mysteries of life require trust in God. Faith brings patience as she waits for answers. It will carry her through a spiritual desert or rut. Faith won't take up much space in her suitcase because a little faith goes a long way. Even a little faith can ignite your daughter's courage—and diminish her fear.

Truths Worth Packing

- "Jesus replied, 'You don't understand now what I am doing, but someday you will.'" (John 13:7)
- "Now faith is confidence in what we hope for and assurance about what we do not see." (Hebrews 11:1 NIV)
- "Afterward the disciples asked Jesus privately, 'Why couldn't we cast out that demon?' 'You don't have enough faith,' Jesus told them. 'I tell you the truth, if you had faith even as small as a mustard seed, you could say to this mountain, "Move from here to there," and it would move. Nothing would be impossible.'" (Matthew 17:19–20)
- "But blessed is the one who trusts in the LORD, whose confidence is in him. They will be like a tree planted by the water that sends out its roots by the stream. It does not fear when heat comes; its leaves are always green. It has no worries in a year of drought and never fails to bear fruit." (Jeremiah 17:7–8 NIV)
- "So we're not giving up. How could we! Even though on the outside it often looks like things are falling apart on us, on the inside, where God is making new life, not a day goes by without his unfolding grace. These hard times are small potatoes compared to the coming good times, the lavish celebration prepared for us. There's far more here than meets the eye. The things we see now are here today, gone tomorrow. But the things we can't see now will last forever." (2 Corinthians 4:16–18 MSG)

Questions to Unpack

1. Have you ever micromanaged a situation that called for patience and trust in God? If so, what did you learn?
2. Name a struggle that led to a new blessing for your daughter. Looking back, where do you see God's hand? How did her struggle affect her faith?
3. Do you believe perfect love casts out fear? Does fear ever dominate your parenting decisions? Explain.

A Prayer to Lighten Your Load

Dear Lord,
Use my daughter and her generation as solutions to our fallen world. Surround them with angels to protect them physically, mentally, emotionally, and spiritually. Give them wisdom beyond their years. I praise You for being a perfect Father. Thank You for loving me even when I fail to trust You. In Jesus' name I pray, amen.

CONCLUSION

*May you live out the hardest parts of your life
with a joyful rebellion against the darkness.*

KATHERINE WOLF

The mayor of a college town was asked what safety advice he gave to his daughter, who had started school on that campus.

He replied, "The main thing I preach to her is safety in numbers. Use the buddy system, especially at night."

The same advice I gave to my daughters when they were young and I dropped them off at a birthday party at the skating rink ("Always stay with a friend, and don't go to the bathroom or anywhere else alone") holds equally true as they grow up.

In some ways this message gets more imperative. Especially as our daughters leave our home, they need friends who have their backs. They need a loyal wingman (or two) who shares their values and truly cares about them. Finding a good wingman begins with *being* a good wingman—being the friend who looks out for others and protects them from ill intent.

Without company like this, we all become easier targets.

In the Air Force and the Navy, the wingman concept is a formal part of culture, as you may know from the *Top Gun* movies.

This dynamic plays out in nature, too, through a phenomenon called a murmuration. A murmuration takes "birds of a feather flock together" to a whole new level. It happens when tens of thousands, sometimes hundreds of thousands, of starlings fly together in unity to create art in the sky.[1] Starlings are very small birds. Alone they make easy prey. But in a murmuration, they make a profound and magnificent statement as they twist, turn, and swoop together. Their group dynamic makes people stop, look up, and marvel.

While every bird is soaring, no birds are colliding. There are no turf wars or egos, just a jaw-dropping miracle of harmony that points to God's power.

I learned about murmurations while visiting Sea Island, Georgia, for a speaking event. Before I flew home, Lucas Ramirez gave me a copy of the book he'd cowritten called *Designed for More: Unleashing Christ's Vision for Unity in a Deeply Divided World*.[2]

I read this book on my trip back to Birmingham, and I couldn't put it down. What a treasure to add to my suitcase—both my physical suitcase that day *and* the spiritual suitcase I carry through life!

A murmuration, Ramirez said, offers a vision for how powerful the church could be if we achieved the unity Jesus prayed for.[3] Imagine a faith community where everyone is soaring, yet nobody is colliding. Everyone is using their unique gifts, yet still harmoniously part of something grander.

Despite our differences, we unite in the love of Christ. We pursue goodness and holiness together. We thrive as we move toward light.

The grand display makes people look up. They're intrigued, and many will want to join the flock. While a starling on the ground looks ordinary, it becomes majestic in the air. We also look majestic when we soar together because we're filled with the Holy Spirit.

Despite our differences, we unite in the love of Christ. We pursue goodness and holiness together. We thrive as we move toward light.

Here's the best part: The main reason why starlings fly in a murmuration is for protection from a common enemy.[4] It's a defense mechanism that leverages the power of relationships.

Alone, starlings don't stand a chance against deadly predators like peregrine falcons, buzzards, and hawks. But together they gain power. The group movements disorient and deter their predators. A falcon can easily attack a single bird, but flying into a horde of starlings is much more difficult.

Starlings are most vulnerable when they isolate. The moment a starling splits off from the flock, it becomes a target. Predators wait to see which starlings wander. When starlings divide, they die. Cohesion brings survival.[5]

Raising empowered daughters in an age of new challenges has many parallels to a murmuration. Consider the following ways that humans are like starlings:

1. We're strongest when we find harmony.
2. We're most vulnerable when we isolate.
3. We have a deadly predator who waits in the wings. He comes to steal, kill, and destroy (John 10:10). He looks for someone to devour (1 Peter 5:8).
4. The Enemy wants division. Unity is our best protection.

5. We're designed to live in close community. Having a strong inner circle, wingmen we deeply trust, moves us in the right direction.

6. When we unite, God is glorified. We create an army of light.

All darkness comes from Satan, and his goal is to destroy God's people. He wants us to feel lonely, stuck, and hopeless. He wants our dark nights to feel darker—and our baggage to feel heavier.

Jesus came to lighten this load. He works miracles when we join forces. As evangelist Vance Havner said, "Christians, like snowflakes, are frail, but when they stick together they can stop traffic."[6] There's no limit to what God can do when we share a common goal.

We'll never be perfect moms. We'll never pack a perfect suitcase. But we can be wise in how we channel our energy and prioritize the ten essentials of raising empowered girls today:

1. Love
2. Truth
3. Integrity
4. Relationship smarts
5. Perspective
6. Discernment
7. Connection
8. Purpose
9. Perseverance
10. Faith

God specifically chose your daughter to live in this moment in time. He intentionally placed your daughter and mine in the same generation.

What if we found strength in numbers?

What if we created an army of light?

What if we looked out for our closest neighbors?

What if we encouraged harmony as our daughters move together toward their Creator?

Ultimately, *this* journey matters most. This journey toward God is what we're preparing our daughters for. He'll create a new order one day of no death, no sorrow, and no pain (Revelation 21:4). Until then, we live in the messy middle. We parent with hope in an age of darkness and help our daughters navigate a broken world.

Our daughters are designed to soar. They need friends who want to soar too. Let's cultivate the roots they need to feel secure— and the wings they need to fly. Let's work mindfully toward the day when they leave our home to serve their generation. Let's pray for every girl to reach her God-given potential and inspire others to do the same.

> In the same way, let your light shine before others, that they may see your good deeds and glorify your Father in heaven.
>
> MATTHEW 5:16 NIV

25 TALKING POINTS FOR HARD CONVERSATIONS

Friend, learning to speak the truth in love is a crucial life skill. Talks with your daughter will always go better when you begin with this goal in mind.

Having hard conversations feels awkward at first, but I encourage you to keep going. Be brave in sharing your family values and setting a baseline of truth.

The world will tell your daughter that "anything goes." It will inundate her with conflicting opinions, demands, and advice. Point her to God when she is unsure. Remind her that He is a God of order and peace, not disorder and confusion (1 Corinthians 14:33). His way makes everything better.

Here are some talking points that I consider important. Take what you want as you decide what messages *you* want to share.

1. **What you put into your body matters.** Whether it's food, alcohol, or drugs, it affects your physical, mental, and spiritual well-being. Love your body, heart, mind, and soul enough to protect them. Make healthy choices that help you feel strong and good about yourself. You only get one body in life, and that body must last you a very long time, so be kind to it. Stay in control, learn the art of moderation, and avoid toxic substances.

2. **You always have a choice.** You don't "have" to do anything you know isn't right. It's okay to leave a party that's getting too wild. It's okay to ditch a date who's being disrespectful. Think for yourself and be a leader, even if that means standing alone. Find your people by noticing who shares your life goals and is headed in the same direction as you.

3. **Boundaries are good, and setting personal boundaries for yourself is crucial.** Especially in college, you can compromise your values without anyone blinking an eye. With nobody to monitor you (making sure you study, go to class, take care of yourself, choose healthy relationships), it's crucial to set personal standards.

   Live within the boundaries of wise freedom. Decide in advance what you will and won't do. If you enter new situations with a *maybe* mindset, thinking, *I'll figure it out when I get there*, you're much more likely to cave or be talked into things you wouldn't normally do.

4. **When you leave home, you become the young woman you're going to be. Your friends play a major role in shaping this person, so choose your most trusted circle wisely.** Choose friends who are fun *and* good for you. Choose friends who

help you live out your convictions, fill in the gap when you're homesick, and become your family away from home.

5. **Take care of your people.** If your friend isn't thinking clearly, then think clearly for her. This may mean not letting her walk home alone at night; pulling her back before she leaves the bar with a stranger; or calling her parents when she has a serious problem that needs intervention.

   Love your friends as you hope they'll love you. Don't be scared to seek help if someone's health or life is on the line. Most states have a Good Samaritan law that offers legal protection to those who assist in good faith during an emergency like a drug overdose or an accident.[1] Make safety a top priority, for yourself and others.

6. **Every choice has a consequence, and in your teenage years, your choices begin to have long-term consequences.** Even at age thirteen, a mean, lewd, or inappropriate post on social media could destroy your future chance of getting into the company, university, or sorority of your dreams. A DUI can keep you out of law school. You'll reap what you sow, so make good choices that will pay off later. Don't jeopardize your future by acting impulsively.

7. **If you make one bad choice, don't follow up with a second bad choice.** An example of this is getting drunk at a party and then deciding to drive. Call someone after your first mistake. Don't keep going and make a bad situation worse. Dr. Lisa Damour said, "Call me if things get out of hand. I will never make you sorry that you asked for my help."[2]

8. **A few steps in the wrong direction can lead to more steps in the wrong direction.** Just a two-degree change in your lifestyle can ultimately land you in a place you never intended

to be. If you make a dumb move—like cheating on a test, yelling at a friend, or skipping work—learn from it. Don't repeat the mistake or let it become a pattern that's hard to reverse.

9. **Learn how to say no—and don't let anyone push you to act against your better judgment.** No matter how charming, popular, or attractive someone is, they are bad news if they ask you for anything inappropriate, like a nude picture. You don't need them in your life, so don't give them the time of day. The best people set a high bar for themselves and don't put you in a compromising position. Ignore the bad seeds and know that manipulators take the path of least resistance. They like people who are easy to persuade and have a hard time saying no.

10. **God's grace is bigger than any mistake. Your mistakes don't define you.** If you wake up one day and can't believe what you've done or who you've become, ask God to forgive you and help you start over. Turn the page and know that you're allowed to reinvent yourself.

    God's mercies are new each morning, and through Christ you can become a new creation (Lamentations 3:22–23; 2 Corinthians 5:17). Who you're becoming today matters more than who you've been in the past. Don't let the Enemy get in your head and convince you that it's too late to change. Jesus came to save us as sinners, not as saints.

11. **Your young adult years are a time to either neglect your faith or take your faith to a new level.** Taking it to a new level gives you an anchor for life's storms. It brings you stability and security. With everything in your life constantly changing—your body, relationships, circumstances, social

life, and more—you can always find peace in a perfect God. On good days, faith can feel like a bonus. But on bad days, it's a lifeline.

12. **God is working in you, giving you the power and the desire to do what pleases Him (Philippians 2:13).** Pay attention to what brings you peace and ignites your passion. What calms your heart? What breaks your heart? What gets you fired up? What inspires the best version of you? If your heart is open, God will energize you to carry out His will. The closer you get to Him, the more your desires will align with His desires—and the more peace you'll have.

13. **Loneliness can sneak up at odd times, especially when you leave home and miss the familiarity of your old life.** Growing pains are normal, so don't isolate yourself or mistakenly believe that nobody understands. God created you to live in community, and when you share your struggles with trustworthy people (like the girls ahead of you who can assure you that you'll find your place), you build deeper, more authentic relationships.

We all feel lonely at times because our journeys are unique. Talking this out helps you feel less alone. It allows God to comfort you so you can comfort others (2 Corinthians 1:4). This gives purpose to your pain. It proves that nothing is wasted in God's greater story, not even loneliness.

14. **When you face a dark season, remember: Suicide is always a terrible idea. Seek help immediately if you ever entertain this notion. Don't struggle alone.** We can walk with you through any problem, and we can help you recover from a major blow—but *you must be here* to do that. Suicide is the only

thing we can't recover from. It's a permanent decision to a temporary problem.

Dark thoughts aren't from God because God created you for a purpose. Your life is priceless, and you matter! Whatever you face, we'll survive it together. Nothing is bigger than my love for you. Nothing is worth taking your life. When you feel hopeless, fight your way back to the light. Let your loved ones help you, and surround yourself with people who restore your hope and faith in yourself.

15. **God won't let you be tempted beyond what you can bear (1 Corinthians 10:13).** So when a hard situation tempts you, pray for a way out. Pray for the strength to walk away, and get comfortable with being uncomfortable. A moment of pleasure isn't worth a lifetime of regret. Just one impulsive decision can drastically alter your life.

16. **God created sex for marriage, and in that context, sex is holy and good.** It's a glue that bonds a husband and wife. But outside marriage, sex leaves scars. It glues you to the wrong person.

When girls choose to be sexually active, they often get clingy and insecure, especially after an argument with their boyfriend, because there's no commitment to keep him from leaving. Dating like you're married makes the breakup feel like a divorce. It's hard to be friends again.

I've never heard a grown woman say, "I'm so glad I had sex with my high school boyfriend!" This choice typically brings regret, so pray for God's help to save this gift for your husband. And for a girl or a boy who's already had sex, there is grace. God can help them choose differently moving forward. He can help them break free from that cycle.

Remember this too: Dating brings rejection. The purpose of dating is to find the *one* person you're meant to marry, and the majority of people don't marry their first romantic interest. Knowing this eases the sting of rejection. It's a good reminder to keep your relationships innocent because only the last boy you date will be your husband. Let your relationships teach you what you do and don't want in a spouse. Aim to end on good terms when possible.

It's always smart to exit a relationship with dignity—and let your ex remember you as "the one who got away" rather than the one he never cares to see again. Be sad at home and cry with your friends, but in public, act dignified. Don't burst into tears, exact revenge, do things that make you look bad, or let the breakup consume you. It won't happen immediately, but you and your ex may be friends again one day if you don't come undone. If that's out of the question, be cordial. Don't burn bridges, because people come back into your life when you least expect it. Acting maturely now will save your future self from feeling mortified when you cross paths with your ex-boyfriend again.

17. **A boy may be part of God's plan for you, but he'll never be The Plan.** Boys make terrible gods, and putting a boy on a pedestal puts unfair pressure on him and sets you up for disappointment.

Boys will come and go, but God is forever, so make Him your number one. Chase your dreams and create an amazing life. If marriage is part of God's plan for you, this will attract the right guys, guys who notice you and think, *Wow. She's awesome. I want to know her better. I'd like to be part of her world.* If marriage isn't part of God's plan for you, you can still be happy and fulfilled. Our world is full of single women who build deep friendships and feel an enormous sense of purpose.

18. **The best romances have a strong friendship too.** Chemistry without friendship will fizzle, and any relationship that stays centered around physical attraction will fail once the novelty wears off and someone more attractive or appealing comes along.

   If physical attraction is all you have with a boy, you make yourself replaceable. Finding physical attraction is easy, but finding physical attraction *plus* a deep spiritual connection is rare and special.

   Approach boys as potential friends, not potential boyfriends. This will keep you from acting fake and free you to be yourself. It also sets you up for a successful marriage, if that is part of God's plan, since friendship is another glue that every marriage needs.

19. **Boys tend to fall into two categories: protectors and predators.** On the surface they can look similar, so be slow to trust. You need more than a few interactions to truly gauge someone's character. Two boys can see the same situation yet have opposite responses. While a protector treats girls like a sister, a predator sees girls as opportunities.

   Two college boys, for instance, walked into an apartment one night and saw a drunk girl passed out on the floor. One boy started to take advantage of her, but thankfully, his friend got angry and pulled him back. Having a moral code gave him a very different view of this stranger. It saved this girl from a lifetime of trauma.

Predators often prey on girls who they think they can conquer. It might be a girl who is young and naive. A girl separated from her friends. An overserved girl at the bar. A girl so starved for male attention that she's easy to coerce. Some predators are attractive, and it could be a cute boy from your class, your friend's brother, or even someone's father who doesn't have your best interest in mind.

Sexual assault is never your fault, and I pray it never happens to you. If it does, don't be ashamed to seek help and tell us. Don't blame yourself for a boy's terrible choices because that is on *him*. Decent humans live by a moral code. They don't use girls, especially vulnerable ones. Only protectors deserve a place in your circle. These are the guys worth knowing and marrying.

20. **All that glitters is not gold.** At some point, you'll be disillusioned. You'll discover that someone or something you adore was all a facade or a sham.

    Value character over charisma and substance over show. Don't get so enamored by wealth, glamour, power, or an impressive lifestyle that you miss what's below the surface. The A-list crowd that looks really fun could be a lion's den. It might not be what you think.

21. **Your gut thinks faster than your brain, so if a situation doesn't feel right, it's probably not right. Again, trust your gut.** In self-defense classes, the first lesson they teach relates to situational awareness. Making eye contact, being aware of your surroundings, and having your wits about you makes you less appealing as a target. You're less likely to be attacked if you can identify a perpetrator in a lineup.

    So keep your head on a swivel. Choose a different path if

someone gives you an odd vibe. Don't let anyone guilt-trip you by calling you names. When it comes to safety, you can ignore someone and be rude. And if you get attacked, all bets are off. You can kick, scream, punch, and take it up a notch from whatever they do. Don't let them take you to another location. Go down fighting and make it clear that they chose the wrong girl.

22. **When you're at a party or a bar, never leave your drink unattended or take a drink from someone you don't know well, not even a Coke.** Sadly, girls' drinks often get drugged, and it can happen when you're holding a drink and someone sneaks in a pill. Most older girls can tell you a story about it happening to them or a friend.

Date rape drugs make sexual assault easier by making a girl more compliant, weakening her resistance and ability to fight, making her partly or fully unconscious, and lessening her inhibitions so she consents to sex that she normally wouldn't allow.[3] Signs that a girl has been drugged include vomiting, a dazed look in her eyes, loss of consciousness, remembering nothing after taking a drink, confusion, disorientation, and waking up with no recollection of how she got to a new location.[4]

To protect yourself, practice the buddy system. Share your location with friends before you go out. And if someone gets drugged, seek medical help immediately. Get her to a safe place.

23. **There's no such thing as a safe drug. Just because marijuana is legal in some states doesn't mean it's beneficial.** In fact, the opposite is true. Today's marijuana is many times more potent as strains from thirty years ago, and more teens who

use marijuana now suffer from psychosis.[5] Having one psychotic episode after cannabis use creates a 47 percent chance of developing schizophrenia or bipolar disorder, and that risk is highest for teens and young adults.[6]

Your brain is less resilient than an adult brain because it's still maturing. You're more prone to addiction, and nine out of ten drug addicts say they first used drugs before age eighteen.[7] As the author of *The Teenage Brain* said, "The earlier the use, the greater the abuse."[8] Legal and safe are *not* the same thing, and there is great evidence that marijuana hurts the developing brain.[9]

Also, any drug not from a pharmacy, even a sleeping pill from a friend, could contain fentanyl. Fentanyl is lethal in tiny amounts, equivalent to five to seven grains of salt, and you never know which pills in a batch contain a little too much.

Drug dealers have smuggled frightening amounts of fentanyl across America's borders. From September 2022 to September 2023 alone, enough fentanyl was seized at the US border to kill every American eighteen times.[10] Almost 110,000 Americans died from a drug overdose in 2022, mainly due to fentanyl.[11]

Even first-time drug users have died because of fentanyl. Your life is too valuable to take that risk, so avoid drugs completely. Remember that just one pill can kill.

24. **Pornography thrives on novelty. The addictions get more perverse over time because it takes more to get the same high.** Our world has normalized pornography. Everything is hypersexualized, and perverse music videos and fashion campaigns now get touted as art and entertainment.

But pornography rewires the brain and sexual response. It feeds a desire for counterfeit sex and ruins dating, romance, and marriage.

Many young men, strong Christians included, face devastating heartache as they marry the love of their life— and then can't perform physically in the bedroom because their brain is hooked on porn. If someone had warned them about this consequence of porn, they may have fought their addiction rather than accepted it. They may have questioned their habit.

Ask God to protect you and your future husband from pornography. If you stumble across it or feel like you have a problem, tell us so we can help. I won't judge you or anyone else, because there is a multibillion-dollar industry trying to get you hooked. Evil is always a parasite of the good,[12] and pornography takes a good gift created by God and corrupts it.

Also, any guy who expects you to accept his porn addiction isn't the right person to date or marry. Left unchecked, his problem will get worse, and your self-esteem will suffer. God has a better plan in mind. He helps us fight addictions that rob us of a beautiful life.

25. **You must want a great life for yourself more than I want it for you.** Ultimately, your life is your own. I can share advice all day, but in the end, you'll make your own decisions and live with the consequences. I'm always here to talk, and I'll always love you. I'd lay down my life for you, and I thank God for choosing me to be your mom.

ACKNOWLEDGMENTS

A friend of mine once explained to me how there are two types of people in this world.

The first type is savvy and street smart. You could put them in a forest without a map, and they'd find their way out. They have a gift for navigating new territory with great success.

The second type is a strong learner. They're smart, too, but if you put them in a forest, they'd need help getting out. With a little experience, however, they could navigate the wilderness better. They just need to get their bearings first.

As the fourth child in my family, I've always fallen into the second category. I grew up watching my older siblings and learning through observation which way I should go. If you and I got lost in a forest together, I'm not the girl to lead you out. I'd never make it on a show like *Survivor*. But if someone older and wiser gives me a lay of the land, I can build on that. I can take their lessons and run.

This analogy kept coming to mind as I wrote this book. Parenting constantly throws us into new territory and new situations—and I've felt lost more times than I can count. I've had to rely on people I trust who know the way better than me. I've wasted time on wrong turns and detours. I've discovered that getting it wrong is often the path to finally getting it right.

In short, I do better when I know the lay of the land rather than go in blindly.

It's with that heart that I wrote this book for you moms behind me. When I meet you at my events, I notice that you're smart and hungry for guidance. You're my fastest growing audience on Instagram and the primary listeners of my podcast. You read books like *Love Her Well*—which I wrote for moms of teenagers— even though your daughter is seven, and you'll do anything to help your child. You like to research and feel prepared, yet this habit can make you feel overwhelmed with all the conflicting advice out there.

Above all things, I encourage you to trust God's voice. Notice what brings you peace. Far more important than my words or the words of any human is the comforting truth of Scripture. It stands the test of time and will never fail you. Your journey is unique, and though your experiences look different from mine, it's an honor to encourage you. Thank you for taking the time to read this book. Thank you for letting me have a small voice in your family's story.

Let me also thank these people who helped get this book in your hands:

My agent, Andrew Wolgemuth, who I can always count on for integrity and good judgment. You've been a huge blessing in my author journey, and I'm so thankful for your guidance, encouragement, and character as we launch our sixth book together. I look forward to launching more!

My amazing team at W Publishing / Thomas Nelson: Brooke Hill, Lauren Bridges, Katherine Hudencial, Elizabeth Hawkins, Carrie Marrs, and Damon Reiss. A special thanks to Brooke (and to Jennifer Stair) for sharpening, strengthening, and organizing the manuscript. This book took a village, and your edits elevated the message and enhanced its relevance. It's been a joy to work with you.

My priest, Father Bob Sullivan, for your wisdom and the way you articulate God that makes people love Him more. Thank you for every manuscript you've reviewed and every question you've answered. You're the best, and our family has been incredibly blessed by you.

My dad, my biggest cheerleader and greatest faith influence. I love you, and I hope that one day, my children's memories of me are as powerful as the memories I have of you.

My husband, Harry, and our four girls: Ella, Sophie, Marie Claire, and Camille. You bring me the greatest joy and offer the most convincing proof of God's goodness to me. Thank you for loving me and supporting me. It's not always easy living with a writer (especially one with a deadline!), but your encouragement and prayers have carried me. I adore each of you and absolutely treasure our family.

Most importantly, I thank You, Lord, for Your faithfulness. Thank You for sustaining me as I finished this manuscript that was my longest and hardest one yet. Please bless every mom who reads it. Keep our eyes fixed on You, and fill our hearts with the hope of what is still to come. Amen.

NOTES

Introduction

1. C. S. Lewis, *Perelandra: A Novel* (Scribner, 2003), 100.
2. Cynthia Yanoff, *Life Is Messy, God Is Good* (Esther Press, 2024), 61.

Chapter 1

1. Dr. Meg Meeker, *Raising a Strong Daughter in a Toxic Culture* (Regnery Publishing, 2020), xiii.
2. Kari Kampakis, "Children Are Blessings, Not Burdens," Karikampakis.com, August 13, 2013, https://www.karikampakis .com/2013/08/children-are-blessings-not-burdens/.

Chapter 2

1. Kari Kampakis, "10 Truths Middle Schoolers Should Know," Karikampakis.com, August 5, 2015, https://www.karikampakis .com/2015/08/10-truths-middle-schoolers-should-know/.
2. Tiffany Wismer, "Teen Boys a Target for Online Exploitation and Sextortion," Fox21 News, March 14, 2024, https://www .fox21news.com/human-trafficking-prevention/teen-boys-a -target-for-online-exploitation-and-sextortion/.
3. Caitlynn Peetz, "Kids' Declining Mental Health Is the 'Crisis of Our Time,' Surgeon General Says," *Education Weekly*, April 25, 2023, https://www.edweek.org/leadership/kids-declining-mental -health-is-the-crisis-of-our-time-surgeon-general-says/2023/04.
4. Jonathan Haidt (@jonathanhaidt), "The 4 New Norms,"

Instagram, April 7, 2024, https://www.instagram.com/p
/C5eUodJOAm3/?img_index=1.

5. Parija Kavilanz, "The 'Sephora Kid' Trend Shows Tweens Are
Psyched About Skincare. But Their Overzealous Approach Is
Raising Concerns," CNN, March 12, 2024, https://www.cnn.com
/2024/03/12/business/sephora-kid-tweens-skincare-obsession
/index.html.

6. Saint Augustine of Hippo, *Confessions*, trans. E. B. Pusey
(Edward Bouverie), book 1, line 4, https://www.gutenberg.org
/files/3296/3296-h/3296-h.htm.

7. Rachel Fleit, director, *Bama Rush* (HBO Max, 2023).

8. Mark Shea, "The Opposite of Love . . . ," *National Catholic
Register*, June 22, 2011, https://www.ncregister.com/blog/the
-opposite-of-love.

9. Tracy Munsil, "Most US Parents Have No Plan for Kids'
Spiritual Development, Research Finds," Arizona Christian
University, September 6, 2023, https://www.arizonachristian.edu
/2023/09/06/most-us-parents-have-no-plan-for-kids-spiritual
-development.

Chapter 3

1. Jean M. Twenge and W. Keith Campbell, *The Narcissism
Epidemic: Living in the Age of Entitlement* (Atria Books, 2009).

2. Madeline Levine, *The Price of Privilege: How Parental Pressure
and Material Advantage Are Creating a Generation of Disconnected
and Unhappy Kids* (HarperCollins Publishers, 2008), 84–85.

3. Joyce Landorf Heatherley, *Balcony People* (Balcony Publishing,
1984), 40.

Chapter 4

1. C. S. Lewis, *Mere Christianity* (Touchstone, 1996), 74–75.

2. Andy Stanley (@AndyStanley), "Don't trade your future,"
X, December 20, 2017, https://x.com/AndyStanley/status
/943525837030215680.

3. David Thomas, *Raising Emotionally Strong Boys* (Bethany House, 2022), 116.

4. Tim Keller (@TimKellerNYC), "Like a surgeon, true friends," Facebook, July 5, 2022, https://www.facebook.com/share/p /1FeW6CZai1/.

5. Robert Fulghum, *It Was on Fire When I Lay Down on It* (Ivy Books, 1991), 102.

Chapter 5

1. David Thomas, *Raising Emotionally Strong Boys* (Bethany House, 2022), 29–30.

2. Corrie ten Boom, *The Hiding Place* (Chosen Books, 1984), 206–7, 210, 220.

3. Rich Karlgaard, *Late Bloomers: The Hidden Strengths of Learning and Succeeding at Your Own Pace* (Currency Books, 2019), 30–31.

4. Sissy Goff, *Brave: A Teen Girl's Guide to Beating Worry and Anxiety* (Bethany House, 2021).

5. Sissy Goff, *The Worry-Free Parent: Living in Confidence So Your Kids Can Too* (Bethany House, 2023), 172.

6. Aundi Kolber, *Try Softer: A Fresh Approach to Move Us Out of Anxiety, Stress, and Survival Mode—and Into a Life of Connection and Joy* (Tyndale, 2020), 61–62.

7. "Dyslexia Is a Superpower: Famous People with Dyslexia," The Dyslexia Code, January 11, 2024, https://thedyslexiacode.com /blog/f/dyslexia-can-be-a-superpower.

8. Gary Caster, *Prayer Everywhere: The Spiritual Life Made Simple* (Franciscan Media, 2018), 61.

9. Jonathan Pokluda (@jpokluda), "At any given moment of your life," Instagram, April 28, 2024, https://www.instagram.com/p /C6UA7Jsrkfb/.

10. Daniel P. Johnson and Mark A. Whisman, "Gender Differences in Rumination: A Meta-Analysis," *Personality and Individual Differences* 55, no. 4 (2013): 367–74, https://doi.org/10.1016/j.paid .2013.03.019.

11. Christine Caine (@ChristineCaine), "Don't allow what has been done to you," X, October 12, 2014, https://x.com/ChristineCaine/status/521377792899174400.

12. Dr. David Jeremiah (Turning Point with Dr. David Jeremiah), "The evidence of God's goodness," Facebook, April 22, 2015, https://www.facebook.com/drdavidjeremiah/photos/a.460094339533/10153214798604534/?type=3.

13. Tim Elmore, "Is Everyone a Leader?," *Psychology Today*, February 20, 2014, https://www.psychologytoday.com/intl/blog/artificial-maturity/201402/is-everyone-a-leader.

Chapter 6

1. Dr. Henry Cloud and Dr. John Townsend, *Boundaries* (Zondervan, 2002), 234.

2. Wayne Gretzky, quoted in Houston Mitchell, "Steve Jobs Used Wayne Gretzky as Inspiration," *Los Angeles Times*, October 6, 2011, https://www.latimes.com/archives/blogs/sports-now/story/2011-10-06/steve-jobs-used-wayne-gretzky-as-inspiration.

3. Priscilla Shirer, *The Armor of God Bible Study* (Lifeway Press, 2015), 11.

4. Shirer, *The Armor of God*, 12.

5. Birds & Bees (@birds_bees), "Want to know more about the drip, drip, drip method," Instagram, January 16, 2023, https://www.instagram.com/birds__bees/p/CngCptOMYgR/?img_index=1.

Chapter 7

1. Fortesa Latifi, "Why So Many Young People Are Cutting Off Their Parents," *Cosmopolitan*, June 22, 2023, https://www.cosmopolitan.com/lifestyle/a44178122/family-estrangement-cut-off-parents/.

2. Gary Smalley, *The Key to Your Child's Heart* (Thomas Nelson, 1992), 5–6.

3. Jim Burns, *Doing Life with Your Adult Children: Keep Your Mouth Shut and the Welcome Mat Out* (Zondervan, 2019), 48–49.

4. Burns, *Doing Life with Your Adult Children*, 115.
5. Restore Ministries (@restore_ministries), "Religion: 'I messed up,'" Instagram, July 19, 2021, https://www.instagram.com/p/CRhgYbnrD32/.
6. "What Is the Circle of Security?," Circle of Security International, accessed December 11, 2024, https://www.circleofsecurityinternational.com/circle-of-security-model/what-is-the-circle-of-security/.
7. Lisa Damour, *The Emotional Lives of Teenagers: Raising Connected, Capable, and Compassionate Adolescents* (Ballantine Books, 2023), 20.
8. Burns, *Doing Life with Your Adult Children*, 44.
9. Burns, *Doing Life with Your Adult Children*, 26, 32, 44–45.

Chapter 8

1. Natural High, https://www.naturalhigh.org/.
2. Bethany Hamilton Network, https://bethanyhamilton.com/blog/heart-behind-ohana-experience.
3. "About Us," Natural High, accessed December 11, 2024, https://www.naturalhigh.org/about/.
4. "About Us," Natural High.
5. Eugene Peterson, *A Long Obedience in the Same Direction: Discipleship in an Instant Society* (InterVarsity Press, 2000).
6. Rick Warren, *The Purpose Driven Life: What on Earth Am I Here For?* (Zondervan, 2013), 109.
7. Kerry Walters, "Mother Teresa: A Saint Who Conquered Darkness," *St. Anthony Messenger*, Franciscan Media, September 2018, https://www.franciscanmedia.org/st-anthony-messenger/mother-teresa-a-saint-who-conquered-darkness/.
8. Rachelle Dragani, "The 25 Most Powerful Women of the Past Century," *TIME*, November 18, 2010, https://content.time.com/time/specials/packages/article/0,28804,2029774_2029776_2031844,00.html.
9. Ryan McGrath, "The Power of Drive: Why It Matters More

Than Motivation and How to Cultivate It," *Forbes*, March 27, 2023, https://www.forbes.com/councils/forbesbusinesscouncil /2023/03/27/the-power-of-drive-why-it-matters-more-than -motivation-and-how-to-cultivate-it/.

10. Tim Keller, *The Prodigal God: Recovering the Heart of the Christian Faith* (Riverhead Books, 2011), 127.

11. Daniel de Visé, "Churchgoing and Belief in God Stand at Historic Lows, Despite a Megachurch Surge," The Hill, December 21, 2022, https://thehill.com/changing-america/enrichment/arts -culture/3782032-churchgoing-and-belief-in-god-stand-at -historic-lows-despite-a-megachurch-surge/.

12. Tim Tebow, quoted in Kameron Brown, "Orlean Beeson School of Education Hosts an Evening with Tim Tebow, Inspiring Students and Support for Scholarships," Samford University, March 15, 2023, https://www.samford.edu/education/news/2023 /School-of-Education-Hosts-Evening-with-Tim-Tebow-Inspiring -Students-and-Support-for-Scholarships.

Chapter 9

1. Adam Grant, *Hidden Potential: The Science of Achieving Greater Things* (Viking, 2023), 67.

2. Tim Keller and Kathy Keller, *The Meaning of Marriage: Facing the Complexities of Commitment with the Wisdom of God* (Riverhead Books, 2011), 17.

3. Corrie ten Boom, *The Hiding Place* (Chosen Books, 1984), 43–44.

4. Kari Kampakis, host, *Girl Mom Podcast*, episode 75, "The Thrill of Hope (with Nashville's Farrell Mason)," November 12, 2023, https://podcasts.apple.com/us/podcast/ep-75-the-thrill-of-hope -with-nashvilles-farrell-mason/id1504764007?i=1000634574072.

5. Scott Stump, "Jenna Says Her Dad's Reaction to Underage Drinking Incident Taught Her About Parenting," *TODAY*, March 10, 2020, https://www.today.com/parents/jenna-bush -hager-underage-drinking-talk-george-w-bush-t175660.

6. Jack Shonkoff, in Bari Walsh, "The Science of Resilience,"

Harvard Graduate School of Education, March 23, 2015, https://
www.gse.harvard.edu/ideas/usable-knowledge/15/03/science
-resilience.

Chapter 10

1. Squire Rushnell coined this term in his Godwink book series,
   https://www.simonandschuster.com/series/The-Godwink
   -Series.
2. Thornton Wilder, *The Eighth Day* (1967), as mentioned in Harold
   Kushner, *When Bad Things Happen to Good People* (Anchor,
   2004), 21–22.
3. "Pray and Don't Lose Heart: What St. Monica Teaches Us About
   Persistence in Prayer," Catholic Diocese of Tyler, August 26, 2021,
   https://www.dioceseoftyler.org/2021/08/26/pray-and-dont-lose
   -heart-what-st-monica-teaches-us-about-persistence-in-prayer/;
   "Writings of St. Augustine," Augustinians of the Province of
   Australasia, accessed December 12, 2024, https://www.osa.org.au
   /resources/writings-of-st-augustine/.
4. Kenneth Johnson, "U.S. Births Remain Near 40-Year Low
   for Third Consecutive Year," Carsey School of Public Policy,
   University of New Hampshire, June 5, 2023, https://carsey
   .unh.edu/publication/us-births-remain-near-40-year-low-third
   -consecutive-year.
5. Jonathan Pokluda, host, *Becoming Something with Jonathan
   Pokluda*, podcast, episode 225, "Should I Want to Have Kids?
   And How Many?", July 30, 2023, https://podcasts.apple.com/us
   /podcast/episode-225-should-i-want-to-have-kids-and-how-many
   /id1454045768?i=1000622869241.

Conclusion

1. Gege Li, "Thousands of Starlings Fly Together to Make an
   Enormous Bird," *New Scientist*, March 17, 2021, https://www
   .newscientist.com/article/mg24933262-500-thousands-of
   -starlings-fly-together-to-make-an-enormous-bird/.

2. Lucas Ramirez with Mike Devito, *Designed for More: Unleashing Christ's Vision for Unity in a Deeply Divided World* (FaithWords, 2018).

3. Ramirez, *Designed for More*, 6.

4. Li, "Thousands of Starlings Fly Together."

5. Ramirez, *Designed for More*, 7, 95, 153.

6. Vance Havner, quoted in Rick Warren, *The Purpose Driven Life* (Zondervan, 2013), 275.

Appendix

1. For more information on your state's Good Samaritan law, see https://www.safeproject.us/good-samaritan-laws/.

2. Lisa Damour (@lisa.damour), "Call me if things," Instagram, August 6, 2024, https://www.instagram.com/p/C-Vw--cwyRVG/?img_index=4.

3. Zawn Villines, "What You Should Know About Date Rape Drugs," Medical News Today, October 26, 2023, https://www.medicalnewstoday.com/articles/320409.

4. Villines, "What You Should Know About Date Rape Drugs."

5. Julie Wernau, "More Teens Who Use Marijuana Are Suffering from Psychosis," *Wall Street Journal*, January 10, 2024, https://www.wsj.com/us-news/marijuana-depression-psychosis-869490d1.

6. Wernau, "More Teens Who Use Marijuana."

7. "National Substance Abuse Prevention Month," The National Child Traumatic Stress Network, accessed December 13, 2024, https://www.nctsn.org/resources/public-awareness/national-substance-abuse-prevention-month.

8. Frances E. Jensen, *The Teenage Brain: A Neuroscientist's Survival Guide to Raising Adolescents and Young Adults* (HarperCollins, 2015), 150–68.

9. Joanna Jacobus and Susan F. Tapert, "Effects of Cannabis on the Adolescent Brain," *Current Pharmaceutical Design*

20, no. 13 (2014): 2186–93, http://dx.doi.org/10.2174
/13816128113199990426.

10. Anna Giaritelli, "Enough Fentanyl Stopped at Border in Past
Year to Kill Every American 18 Times," *Washington Examiner*,
October 21, 2023, https://www.washingtonexaminer.com/news
/2719723/enough-fentanyl-stopped-at-border-in-past-year-to-kill
-every-american-18-times/.

11. Brian Mann, "U.S. Drug Overdose Deaths Hit a Record
in 2022 as Some States See a Big Surge," NPR, May 18,
2023, https://www.npr.org/2023/05/18/1176830906/
overdose-death-2022-record.

12. Bishop Robert Barron, "The Parasite of Evil," Word on Fire,
July 23, 2023, https://www.wordonfire.org/videos/sermons/the
-parasite-of-evil/.

ABOUT THE AUTHOR

Kari Kampakis is an author, podcaster, and national speaker from Birmingham, Alabama. Her bestselling books for moms, *Love Her Well* and *More Than a Mom*, and books for teenage girls, *Yours, Not Hers*, *10 Ultimate Truths Girls Should Know*, and *Liked*, have been used widely across the country for small group studies.

Kari's work has been featured on Focus on the Family, the Bethany Hamilton Network, *TODAY*, *Live in Love* with Annie Downs and Lauren Akins, *Raising Boys and Girls*, *Live with the Louhs*, EWTN, Yahoo! News, Grown & Flown, Christian Parenting, and other national outlets. She also hosts the *Girl Mom* podcast. Kari and her husband, Harry, have four daughters and a dog named Lola. Visit www.karikampakis.com or find Kari on Instagram, Substack, and Facebook.